EVERY ROSE HAS
ITS THORN

EVERY ROSE HAS ITS THORN

A THORN IN THE FLESH

SYDNEY ROSE RADECKI

Palmer,

thank you so much for
all of your support! It
means the world to me!

Sydney Rose Radecki

NEW DEGREE PRESS

EVERY ROSE HAS ITS THORN

A Thorn in the Flesh

ISBN   978-1-64137-411-8 *Paperback*

978-1-64137-412-5 *Kindle Ebook*

978-1-64137-413-2 *Digital Ebook*

I dedicate this book to the fighters, the warriors, the ones who have a silent struggle, the ones who need hope, the ones who lack, and the ones who have a thorn in the flesh.

CONTENTS

———

We are not defined by our thorns. We are defined by our heart, mind, and faith. Not the thorns that stick through them.

INTRODUCTION

DEDICATION AND LETTER TO READERS

This book is dedicated to all those who struggle, who fear, who climb, and who do the unimaginable through suffering, which often goes unnoticed and unseen. Anxiety, depression, and OCD are all overused but under-appreciated words. Some people say them when they poke fun at a friend who always checks to make sure their front door is locked before bed, or when someone is nervous about a job interview. But to others, like me, these words hold an incredible power—almost control—over life. To some, these abstract concepts become a segment of identity; something that pervades their daily experience. For me, faith was, and still is, instrumental in dealing with my mental health struggles. My hope is that this book will help others like me bridge the gap between mental health and Christianity, forming an airtight coping mechanism and community.

This book is also dedicated in memory of my late great-grandmother, Rose Marie Newsom. Rose Marie, also known as "GG" or "Tootsie," served on the Mental Health Board in

Hartsville, South Carolina. Her passion for mental health education serves as an inspiration today.

Dear readers,

My name is Sydney Radecki, and I am passionate about the education of mental health as well as the development and growth in one's faith. I have learned so much throughout this book-writing process about not only myself but also those around me, and I have a lot prepared at the table for you. You may be reading this introduction wondering what on earth you have in your hands and what you have gotten yourself into, but I fully believe the Lord has guided this book into your hands as a way to aid and heal you.

Before we begin, I would like to share a bit about my own personal journey with mental health and faith.

Freshman year at Clemson University I began to realize that my constant negative feelings were not normal. These feelings were not just warning signs of typical stress or agony about tests.

They were anxiety.

Long story short, I was diagnosed with Generalized Anxiety Disorder in October 2018. When I was diagnosed, I was not surprised and I took it in stride. In all honesty, I was really proud of myself for going to get help when I needed it most. But I know that diagnoses like mine aren't easy for everyone to swallow. Some people have a really difficult time after being diagnosed with a mental health disorder and are too distraught to be proud that they sought out answers.

When I was diagnosed, I knew I had a long journey ahead, but I was very relieved to finally place a real, certain name on the issue at hand. That's what made me feel the best about it, to know what it was. From that point on, I made a point to remember that I am not my anxiety, that just because I have anxiety does not mean it owns me. Furthermore, I trusted in the knowledge that help was on the way, that therapy shouldn't be frowned upon, and that it is always okay to ask for help. I prayed for a good while before I stepped foot into the mental health services office that day. That's likely why I took my diagnosis so well; it was because I had prepared myself mentally but had also called upon a higher power and bigger name to come in and give me peace. That was just one of the many times I have prayed and the Lord has given me peace throughout this journey.

After I went to get the answers to my prayers, the support I received from my parents was incredible. I am still so thankful to them for helping me every step of the way and helping me relax my mind when things got hard. My family and friends have quickly learned what my triggers are as I have learned them. They always provide the most reassuring words, and they always are just a prayer away. They support me no matter what my worry is. Having this support team has enabled me to grow and to learn so much about myself and about how to handle myself during the anxiety-inducing moments. However, I do know that it is not as common as one would hope for some people to receive that level of support, and I have heard stories from some of my friends about how that lack is prevalent.

According to surveys conducted in 2002 by the University of Leicester, around 69 percent of students would be more likely to contact family members and friends about their struggles rather than staff members.[1] This relates to my situation because right off the bat when I was struggling and knew something was wrong, I would reach out and talk to my mom. My mom gave me advice and I tried to work through it, but after talking to my parents about it I decided to go talk to CAPS, the Counseling and Psychology Services on Clemson's campus.

Sometimes it takes me longer than others to quiet my roaring mind down, but no matter what, I can count on the support of my family and friends to pull me back down to earth. One thing I have found about myself is that when I am tired from my hectic schedule, that triggers my anxiety. I have learned that whatever negativity flows through my brain is false, especially when I'm tired and my anxiety is triggered. My family and friends all understand this. My roommates do as well, and they know that if I'm napping in my room that I am doing that as more of a self-care task to keep myself from breaking my own heart.

So with that, here is my first message to you: always reach out for help when you need it. It may not necessarily be with a

---

1   Quinn, N., Wilson, A., MacIntyre, G. and Tinklin, T. (2009). 'People look at you differently': students' experience of mental health support within Higher Education. [online] Taylor & Francis.

mental health issue, but this advice still applies. You are not weak for asking for help, as mental health is as real as any physical or bodily health conditions. Ask for help when you are confused and when you are stuck in a rut. I promise you that it will help you more than you can imagine right now.

When they say it takes a village to raise and develop someone they really mean it: the support I have received from my family, my closest friends, and my sorority sisters means the world to me. I am so thankful for them during every trial and hard time. Each of these people—you all know who you are—believed in me and have enabled me when sometimes I did not believe in myself. Whether you knew about my battle with anxiety or not, you have played an influential part in this story.

Finally, I want you to remember and hold close in your heart that you are never alone. It is, and was, very easy for me to feel like no one understood me because of how warped of a perception of reality I have in my anxious states, but God has proven once again that I am understood and that I am not alone. One statistic that moved me, specifically about Generalized Anxiety Disorder (GAD), comes from Medical News Today: "GAD affects around 6.8 million people in the U.S.—or more than 3 percent of the nation's adults." It is incredibly comforting for me to know that God is using me and all of the rest of the 6.8 million people who suffer from GAD to inspire and to move others, and that He is helping us to not let ourselves be conquered by the lies of anxiety. You are never alone, even when you feel like it; there is always someone out there who may be dealing with a similar thing.

My sweet Grammy has been such a huge influence in my life, especially with regard to my faith walk. I have learned so much from her and she prays for me so much; she has really shown me how to have a heart for others and to keep moving forward despite the obstacles that life throws my way. Every single person who has ventured and crossed paths with me has motivated me to be better and to stay strong despite the struggles that force their way in.

God bless you,

Sydney Radecki

In the interest of education and helping one another, I would like to provide you with some resources just in case you, or someone close to you, needs them.

National Suicide Prevention Lifeline: 800-273-8255 (24/7)

Mental Health Crisis Hotline Number: 888-788-2823 (24/7)

Crisis Text Line: Text SUPPORT to 741-741 (24/7)

CHAPTER 1

THE SHIP

———

Visualize this: you're standing on a ship in the middle of the ocean. Everything is going okay. All of sudden you feel a little jolt. The waves get more and more rough. The water is so rocky that you begin to sway, then you end up moving around, losing your balance. You eventually fall to the ground because of how hard the ship is rocking.

You ask, "God, where are you right now in the midst of trouble?"

God says, "I am the ship. You are not in the ocean right now. Sure, things are a little rough, but I am the ship. You are the passenger. I guide you, and during periods of rocky waves, I carry you through and over them."

During this story, the image of the waves may have you thinking about something close to you that directly impacts you. It may be stress, fear, depression, anxiety, or whatever struggle you have been going through for years.

The most important thing to remember before diving straight into this book loaded with hope, strategies, and stories on how to grow as a Christian, specifically in the midst of mental health issues and trying times, is to look to Him. Think of Him as that ship right there with you, protecting you. You may feel like you are going to be sucked into those jagged icy waves tomorrow, but be still and know that you will not be. You are forever protected, even when the waves threaten otherwise. Be still and know our Lord and Savior, the King of all kings, is with you throughout all of the dark and hard times, even when waves threaten to harm you.

Jeremiah 29:11 NIV: "For I know the plans I have for you, declares the Lord, plans for welfare, and not for evil, to give you hope and a future."[2]

My name is Sydney Radecki. I am a native of South Carolina and a current student at Clemson University. I grew up going to church, but it took me until my freshman year of high school to really get plugged into the word and into a positive community of believers. Through the years, I have gained a lot of incredible insight and wisdom into the world around us, as well as into the Word of God and His grace. I believe it is my duty to spread that wisdom to you, so that is why you are holding this book today.

---

2   Bible Gateway. (2019). *Bible Gateway Passage: Jeremiah 29:11 – New International Version*

Being college students, it feels as though we are being thrown to the wolves. Whether that is going through a tough class, a really difficult break-up, or anything else, it happens to everyone. When it happens, it is extremely easy to lose sight of the One who matters, and it is easy to feel as though you are losing control. This feeling where you think you are losing control is simply terrifying, but in that moment, what matters the most is that you stay true to yourself and to the King and that you cling to Him through all things, just like we see in THE SHIP.

CHRISTIANS HAVE MENTAL HEALTH DISORDERS TOO

Over the years, I have heard so many people talk about Christians as if they couldn't possibly have mental illnesses. And for some reason, I have never heard anyone utter a word about mental health in church or at church gatherings. To me, that does not make sense.

As Christians, we do not have everything all together all of the time. In fact, it is close to impossible to have everything together 100 percent of the time—and if it ever looks like that, be ready for the Lord to shake things up in a good way. People don't really talk about it a lot because they feel as though the two things, meaning faith and mental health, are on opposite poles of the earth, because it is common to think that since God is omnibenevolent, mental disorders should not exist. In this book, I am here to discuss that and to shine a spotlight on these things and how they coincide.

Mental health is a very important thing and it is as important as physical health. It is very real. Just because you may not be able to tell that someone isn't physically sick doesn't mean that they aren't suffering in some way. Mental health disorders are very real and impact people in different ways.

Christians have struggles too! Having a diagnosed mental health disorder is a struggle, but it is mainly due to a chemical imbalance in the brain. Everyone deals with anxiety, doubt, worry, fear, etc. from time to time, but the thing about Christians is that we have different mechanisms and someone to turn to in these times. Someone who we can always rely on, someone who can give us heavenly peace, and someone who knows exactly what we're going through.

Like THE SHIP, we are called to trust the Lord even when things are getting really bad and rough. We are called to trust Him despite the doubts that occur and despite the fear that ensues. Things in life on earth will never be 100 percent perfect, but don't doubt the goodness of our Lord. He is able and He is ready to deliver you from your struggles and to help place you in a better spot.

MY JOURNEY

I began to feel like I was losing control of my life in the first semester of my freshman year of college. I was going through a lot of various things that weren't great, including relationship ordeals and just the overall transition to college. I began to realize my worry and anxious feelings weren't something that I could handle on my own, even after praying and shifting my focus. So, the Lord led me to the on-campus mental health services one day.

The night before my first appointment, everything was going well, and then I got anxious out of nowhere. That is when I realized that I had an issue that needed to be addressed, and I was tired of suffering from it and not getting anywhere. I took to the Internet and scheduled that initial appointment to get answers right away the following morning following my classes.

That next morning, a sunny and beautiful Friday, I went to my appointment. When I got to the building, I physically stopped moving and just stared at the door. I was terrified. I was fearful. Something was pushing me to go back to my dorm and not get the help I needed ... but thankfully, I decided that the Lord put me there for a reason, so I walked through those doors with a little confidence and a lot of faith. I felt like I was in a dream in this moment—I could not believe I was doing what I was doing. My mind was telling me I was fine, and I grew more anxious.

I checked in at the counter and then sat down in a chair and waited until my appointment. Once it was my time, a younger lady called me back and we talked for a while. Once it was time, another woman came into the waiting room and called my name. I followed her to a small, dimly lit office in the back of the Student Health Center. Almost immediately after sitting in a burgundy armchair, I started spilling my story. I told her everything, from my worries about biology class to my boy troubles. As I talked, I felt a weight lifting from my shoulders, as if God were encouraging me to keep going. She concluded that I do have Generalized Anxiety Disorder and I am now medicated for it. I was then sent to a class for four weeks where we talked about stress management and how to cope with stress, anxiety, and depression disorders.

Months later, I can say that I am still so glad that I took the brave stance and went forward and got the help I needed. I still struggle from anxious moments, but I know that I am NOT my disorder and it doesn't define me. It is simply something that I deal with from time to time. I am so grateful that the Lord led me through that day and to my next great challenge in life: realizing mental health is stigmatized and it needs to be talked about.

Just a few months later, I heard about the opportunity to write a book. I immediately chose to write about the intersection of faith and mental health and my personal stories with both, in order to show the intersection between the two. Looking back on the initial diagnosis and this book writing journey, I fully believe it was in God's plan for me to have an anxiety disorder. I believe this for many reasons, and just a couple of them are because it has strengthened me tremendously not only as a person but also in my walk with God, and because I have a story to share with others. I believe it is God's plan for me to go and show the world that it is okay to ask for help and that you are not weird because you have a mental health disorder. It's time to end the stigma, and I believe I am called to be a part of that.

YOU ARE WORTHY, YOU ARE LOVED
Always remember that no matter the mental health issues you go through, you are so worthy and so loved. These illnesses do not define you—you are not your illness. It is something

you struggle with, but always remember that everyone has a unique struggle and you are never alone. I can't begin to stress this enough. You are still so special and so worthy no matter what thoughts go through your head, what you do or don't do, and no matter what you struggle with. There are plenty of people out there who want to talk to you and help you.

While talking about diagnosed mental health disorders, I don't want you to forget that it is normal to be a little anxious, sad, and doubtful from time to time. If you are continuously and sometimes constantly anxious to the point of shaking or having panic attacks, or sad to the point of depression, then definitely seek medical care. If you believe you need help, definitely seek out a medical professional because they will help you and know exactly what to do.

The Lord has given us the privilege of having the doctors, nurses, and therapists to be His hands and feet and to help resolve the earthly pain we commonly feel. It can be a terrifying thing going into an appointment not knowing what to expect, but just know that these individuals want to help you. It is their job, but they are doing it out of the goodness of their hearts, and that is why this is their job.

The Lord designed us to be imperfect, because otherwise we wouldn't need Him. Treat your struggles as something designed to bring you closer to God and to help lead you on your walk with Christ, because it absolutely is that. The Lord would never allow anything to happen to you if He knew it wouldn't shape or mold you in some way, and it all is a part of His plan.

For example, when I would get anxious beyond belief, I would wonder why that was happening to me, but after thinking and just working myself up more about the subject, I would immediately resolve to pray about it. There was a reason why I went through about a month or so of not knowing a solution to my anxiety. It was because the Lord was ultimately working to build endurance in me, and He was working to help mold me into the woman I am today.

EVERYONE'S INNER WARRIOR

It is so important to not shame individuals for their mental health disorder. We commonly see Facebook posts about our friend who can't bring themselves to do the dishes. It's easy to make judgments about how "lazy" or "needy" this person is, but always remember that there could more going on than meets the eye. That person may be battling serious depression and be writing that post to ask for help. Never belittle anyone for their disorder or for their struggles. It's also important to stop expecting people to always reach out for help; rather, it is important to reach in. I once saw a quote about that, and it really moved me because a lot of times it is hard for individuals to reach out. Talk to people and ask how they're doing, build that trust and relationship with them, and then guide them to get the help they need.

Everyone is worthy no matter what their life looks like from the outside, because on the inside I promise you there is a warrior there. A warrior who is working hard despite not feeling like it. A warrior who has pushed themselves some days to just get out of bed. A warrior who just prayed for the first time in years because they realized that that was all they had. A warrior who conquered the fear and went on to get help.

You, too, have that warrior within you. I don't personally know your struggle, but I can promise you this: you are a warrior. On your toughest days you have risen again and pushed forward, by God's grace. The Lord is working in your life more than you realize!

Together we will be tackling some coping methods for mental health disorders and pairing them with a strengthening of faith. I will be sharing interviews and research that I have done to help you bring together these two very important aspects of life. Keep reading to learn from and about:

- My great-great-Uncle Harold who is a World War II veteran who continues to inspire everyone daily with his faith and messages of hope, despite fighting through and witnessing one of the hardest battles in American history.
- Ministers and pastors who have played huge roles in my faith journey and fight against anxiety. By hearing the messages these individuals have to offer, I have been able to grow and to not let anxiety take the reins, but rather have allowed Jesus to take the reins.
- Some of my close friends, such as Maci Bolin who inspires everyone daily through her story of how a past relationship has strengthened her and has allowed God to come into her life and change things.
- What it means to fight a good fight, and how your struggles actually can be considered a good fight. Furthermore, tips on how to make the journey a little more bearable by God's grace.

Remember: you and I are a team here. I am speaking and sharing what the Lord wants you to hear, and the Lord led you to this book for a reason. So, let's dive into the waves.

CHAPTER 2

FEAR IS A LIAR

———

Four words. These four words are so simple, and yet so intricate and powerful. When we think about how fear is a liar, it sparks so much courage and ignites that fire inside of your heart to cast it away. Zach Williams, composer and singer of "Fear Is A Liar," shows us that as long as we declare this statement against the Devil, God will cast out our fears by igniting a fire in our hearts.

Picture this: you're sitting on a sidewalk across from a huge field. In that field you see a man throwing a bunch of brush and dead tree material into a giant pile and igniting it on fire. The fire roars; it grows; it burns. That fire is what it looks like inside our heart, mind, and soul when we let the Lord set our soul free and cast out our fears. It looks bright and it roars.

**

Have you ever had one of those nights when you have been weighed down by your burdens, when you feel as though everything is going in the exact opposite direction that you had planned? Those nights when you just feel like a stick in the mud and you lose all hope?

Well, I understand that, and I want you to know you are not alone.

Time and time again I have prayed, and then have been saved and restored by God's grace. There is one night in particular that sticks out the most to me. I was sitting in the library at school and all of a sudden I got super anxious. Why? It's a little difficult to pinpoint, but it was likely due to stress with schoolwork as well as various things going on in my life. I could feel myself gaining more momentum in a negative way that really threw me off and pushed me around. It was a yucky and terrible feeling, and I knew there was one thing and one thing only that could save me in that moment.

God's grace.

When I tell you that it took every fiber in my body to pray and to ask the Lord to come and help me, I am not kidding. It was a challenge, and I know sometimes it is difficult to talk to God and make your requests known. It was incredibly difficult here. I ended up praying and just needing guidance. Immediately I felt moved to hop on my laptop and look at my Christian music playlist on my Apple Music account. I turned on the playlist and heard a song that has moved me in so many ways: "Fullness" by Elevation Worship.

I heard that song and it helped a lot, but I still knew that I needed more. More, you say? Yes. Of course I did. A song I hadn't heard in a while called "The Hill" by Travis Greene came on. This song moved me beyond belief when I heard it on that day. Travis sang about how there is a cross on the hill with blood on it and that is for me and you. It was so moving to hear how the Lord died on that cross that fateful day and died for us so we could be forgiven for our sins. It helped my anxiety so much and was just the medicine I needed.

From that point on, I felt an overwhelming amount of joy. I knew that what the Lord had in store for my life would be so incredible and fulfilling and that I didn't need to be anxious about anything.

> 1 Peter 5:10 NIV: And the God of all grace, who called you to his eternal glory in Christ, after you have suffered a little while, will himself restore you and make you strong, firm and steadfast.[3]

In life, we deal with various things that break us down. These things cause overwhelming levels of anxiety, doubt, and stress. While these situations cause these negative emotions, it is so reassuring to know that the Lord is allowing us to walk through these things because they are allowing us to grow—not only as people, but also in our faith. It is during these moments in our lives that we realize how much we

---

3   Bible Gateway. (2019). *Bible Gateway Passage: 1 Peter 5:10 – New International Version.* [online]

need Jesus and His grace. It is during these moments when we realize that we can't do it alone—we need His guidance and goodness all of the time. We need this guidance and love all of the time, not just when we are at our lows. We need to celebrate Him always.

My friend, fear is a liar. The devil has put these lies in our minds and has caused so much worry about everything. The devil has caused us to doubt ourselves and one another. Fear not, because fear IS a liar.

We battle these lies and this negativity day in and day out. We hear the awful things that the Devil tries to rope us into believing. It is so essential that we focus on God and give Him our dilemmas and trust that He will bring us through it.

I can't write that it will always be easy to not have fear. If I said that, I would be lying to you. It is not always easy, but I promise you it will always be worth it. Trusting the King of all kings will enable you to grow into a strong human being and Christian.

**

Right now while I am writing this, I am sitting here in a new season of both waiting and finding strength in Christ. A couple of days ago, I prayed that the Lord would give me strength. Boy, he has, but in different ways that I never really expected. I am going through some trials in this season, such as grades and final exams, the unknown of the days coming ahead, and the underlying trials of staying at peace with myself and my situation.

There will always be moments—and even seasons—in your life where you will feel stricken by fear. You will feel trapped and feel like you absolutely have nowhere to run. It's a terrifying feeling, and sometimes it makes you feel lonely. You begin to feel as though everyone is doing so much better than you, and you wonder why you are the one who is struggling.

Isaiah 41:10 NIV[4]: So do not fear, for I am with you; do not be dismayed, for I am your God. I will strengthen you and help you; I will uphold you with my righteous right hand.

I want you to know, my friend, that you are never alone, and you are never the only one going through things. During these panic-induced moments, remind yourself that this too shall pass. It is a very true statement, and while it may take days, weeks, months, or even years to pass, it will pass. Everything will all work itself out, and once you are able to fully see Christ's hand in your situation and how everything has unfolded, you will feel at peace with your life and situation.

To say the phrase FEAR IS A LIAR is such a bold, but true, statement. It is our release of all of that doubt, worry, fear, anxiety, sadness, etc. that is holding us hostage at heart. To be bold with this is to be free, so allow this truth to set you free from the shackles that hold your mind trapped. The song "Fear Is A Liar," composed and performed by Zach Williams, is such a triumphant and bold song that will leave you feeling released from all chains and burdens.

---

4   Bible Gateway. (2019). *Bible Gateway Passage: Isaiah 41:10 – New International Version* [online]

Don't let your fear or burdens hinder you. Keep your guard up but don't let that guard turn into a jail. Like Pastor Steven Furtick of Elevation Church spoke in his message one Sunday, "These doubts and painful situations turn into an invisible prison."[5]

Think about that concept for a second. An invisible prison. It's a prison and you do not even realize you are being held captive! That is how dangerous fear is, and it shows how dangerous your mind truly is. This is where God comes in.

A common theme of mine is that whenever I am at or watching the livestream of Elevation Church, I always take notes because I know that someday I will need to return to them and pull wisdom from them.

Something important that Pastor Steven once said was, "Disappointment can be a portal to your greater purpose, or an invisible prison." In times of these disappointments, it is urgent to allow God to work through your life and to propel you to your next season in life. Disappointments are painful, but it is truly how you react to them that determines everything. That is a truth for everything in life, not just for dealing with disappointments. Your reactions to these hardships, stressful moments, heartbreaks, and generally anything in your life will determine if you are trapped in an invisible prison or not.

---

5   *Flip It | Flip the Flow | Pastor Steven Furtick*. (2019). [video] Directed by S. Furtick. Elevation Church: Elevation Church.

For example, recently if I made an iffy grade on a test, I would try to "Flip The Flow," as Pastor Steven Furtick says, and allow myself to move forward and focus on the opportunity I had to grow. However, a reverse reaction would have caused me to not find my purpose in this moment and to wallow in the sadness of that grade. This negative reaction would have also led me to a period of stress and fear as to what my grades would be like, how this would affect my scholarships, and everything else. That is when I would be trapped in an invisible prison.

In order to grow through your fear and struggles, you have to be willing to experience these negative emotions in the present. Experiencing these emotions will allow the truth to come to you quickly and set you free. The truth will always set you free and the big truth that Jesus tells us is that FEAR IS A LIAR. Of course, it is healthy to have a healthy amount of fear of the Lord because of how mighty He is, but not a high level of fear about general things in your life where you doubt yourself and look down on yourself. It is key to recognize this.

We are not called to have to suffer and stay in these invisible prisons where our hearts are chained and our minds are shackled. We are called to be able to watch the invisible walls of these prisons burn and fall to the ground and to walk out of them and to be able to share our story of victory through our Lord and Savior. We are called to take up the cross and be the soldiers. The ones who bust down walls and help others through these difficulties.

Take the time every day to pray and meditate on what is going on inside your heart and mind. Pray about how things are ravaging, but realize that it is okay. If you start having a case of the "what if's," meaning that you just start questioning yourself and asking what you will do if something happens, then answer those questions. That is so important. Question: "What if I can't do it?" Answer: "I can do it, but if something goes wrong then I will be calm and I won't let the fear of what could happen next take me away. I can do it." Take time to answer your own doubt-filled questions, and take time to pray.

Sometimes it also helps to write things out and to write down the fears that are weighing on your heart. One time I wrote down everything painful that was going on in my life, and then after I wrote it, I tore it to shreds. Why? Because fear is a liar. There is nothing more satisfying than writing down the painful things and then ripping it all to shreds, because you realize that these things do not have as much of a stronghold on your heart anymore.

Don't hesitate to reach out as well; you are never alone. As mentioned before in this chapter, never forget that you are so loved. No one can change that, and God will fill every void in your heart.

END OF CHAPTER TAKEAWAYS SECTION:

BIBLE VERSES FOR REFLECTION:
- 1 Peter 5:10 NIV
- Isaiah 41:10 NIV

QUESTIONS FOR REFLECTION:

- When you have fear in your heart, about anything and everything, what are you going to do to combat it?
- Are you going to allow God in to work even in the midst of your fear? How are you going to do so?

ACTIONABLE TAKEAWAYS:

- Stick sticky notes with positive quotes on your mirror or wall as daily reminders.
- Make time daily for prayer and mediation.

PRAYER:

Heavenly Father, I am ridden with fear and my heart is heavy with the present burdens, past burdens, and potential future burdens. I am fearful about what is to come, and I am unsure of how to move forward without this fear having a total stronghold on me. Father, let Your will be done, and I desire for your grace to come through these false perspectives and fill my heart. Amen.

CHAPTER 3

EVEN IF

———

One night I was about to get onto my laptop, relax and catch up on things. Like most people, I keep a password on my laptop just for added protection so no one can get into my personal items. I was trying to log on and the password would not work. Even though I knew it was the correct password that I had used every single time prior, it still did not work. I got a little frustrated because all I was trying to do was hear God's Word and to absorb a powerful message. It seemed the Lord had other plans.

In times like these, it is very easy to get frustrated about things when they do not quite go your way. It is easy to feel like punching a wall because technology is not working and you feel as though everything is going against your plan. Despite these hard times, it is our duty to cling to the Lord and to trust Him, even if all that is going on is not being able to log into our computers.

It is also in times like these when we can compare ourselves to Job. Job's chapter in the Bible is incredibly powerful because it is especially relatable, but also because we see how

Job persists despite Satan throwing curveballs left and right. Between Job's property being stolen, his children being taken away, and his health failing, he still has unrelenting love for Jesus and for his Heavenly Father.

I have seen many times that the Lord will allow significant, destructive, and massive strikes from the Devil to come in and try to sway us, just as a test of our faith. When you hear that the first time, you may immediately question it and wonder what on earth the Lord is thinking and why such a strike has to happen to us. Believe me, I wonder the same thing, but it is up to us to choose to follow and be a slave to the path of righteousness and all things good.

Again, we see how God loves Job even though Job keeps going through hard times. Just because we go through hard times doesn't mean that God loves us any less; He loves us even if we struggle. Even if we are weak and burdened, He loves us, just like He loves Job.

Returning to my laptop story, this easily could have spiraled out of control. If this had happened months prior, I likely would have gotten very frustrated and agitated. But at that point, I chose to just take a step back, breathe and calm down, and then go on Apple Support and ask for some help. It took a little bit of time, but I eventually received the knowledge I needed to fix this issue. If I had gone the route of frustration and agitation, things would likely look and feel a lot different than they do now.

Sometimes these little strikes could be something bigger for someone else. It may not always be just a faulty computer, or a bad hair day. It could be a diagnosis such as cancer, diabetes, migraines, bipolar disorder, etc. It could be finding out terrible news that shakes you to your core. It could be the fear of the unknown after you submit an application and are awaiting approval, or for the next step.

Oftentimes these strikes will cause some amount of questioning. It could cause us to feel pure anger against God and sometimes question of our own existence, like Job did in Chapter 3 of the Book of Job. Job understandably becomes frustrated with the doubt and confusion that continues to block his path, and the pain that he deals with because of all of the horrid things Satan initiates against him.

We see how Job opens up his heart to us in Chapter 3 by asking God the following:

Job 3:20-23 NIV: Why is light given to those in misery, and life to the bitter of soul, to those who long for death that does not come, who search for it more than for hidden treasure, who are filled with gladness and rejoice when they reach the grave? Why is life given to a man whose way is hidden, whom God has hedged in?[6]

---

6   Bible Gateway. (2019). *Bible Gateway Passage: Job 3:20-23 – New International Version.*

Job, like many of us from time to time, question God and His goodness. When we are in despair, we feel completely unworthy because of the things that are happening, even if we are not at fault. It is during these times that God desires for us to grow in strength and to trust in Him more. Job questions why we should receive this grace and goodness, despite being bitter in our souls at times.

The wrongdoings of others cause this bitterness. The acts of Satan cause this bitterness. God loves us no matter what, despite the rocky waves that pick us up by our feet and throw us to shore. God knows our hearts, and He knows that by grace our hearts can be redeemed from this bitterness. God loves us even if we question Him and His goodness, and He loves us even if we can't always see and understand what He's building us for.

> David 3:17 NIV[7]: If we are thrown into the blazing furnace, the God we serve is able to deliver us from it, and he will deliver us from Your Majesty's hand.

It is through these hard and confusing times that we are called to praise Him instead of to complain. We are called to seek His heart and grab onto his white robe and trust that He will pull us from the fire. He will deliver us, and we will

---

7   Bible Gateway. (2019). *Bible Gateway Passage: Daniel 3:17 – New International Version.*

be saved once again. He is not a God who leaves us stranded, even when we feel like we are.

Finally, we see how the story of Job and his hardships ends up with a happy ending: he is restored. God restored Job and his fortunes, just because Job prayed for his friends when God told him to. From this point, according to Job 42:12 NIV[8]: "The Lord blessed the latter part of Job's life more than the former part. He had fourteen thousand sheep, six thousand camels, a thousand yoke of oxen and a thousand donkeys." He also had seven sons and three daughters. We see how after Job's perseverance and trust, God blessed him in the most unimaginable and incredible ways we could ever imagine as believers.

Think about how mind-blowing that must have been for Job, to all of the sudden see 14,000 sheep, 6,000 camels, 1,000 yoke of oxen, and 1,000 female donkeys all walking up to him. That is quite a visual, and something that just seems impossible, but with God all things are possible. Even if the storm is churning dangerously, even if the ship floor is threatening to cave in, and even if the water is getting high and your mind and heart are racing, God can still do the impossible. You just have to believe, pray, and stay firm in your faith just like Job does.

One of my favorite Christian songs is by the amazing MercyMe, and it is called "Even If." I did a little research and

---

8   Bible Gateway. (2019). *Bible Gateway passage: Job 42:12 – New International Version.*

found an article from The Christian Post[9] about lead singer Bart Millard's reasoning and motivation behind creating such a heart-wrenching and powerful song. Millard's son has had diabetes for almost his whole life, and Millard mentions how being a parent of a child with a chronic illness is a very challenging thing to deal with and manage. His song is a message for the people whose hardships and difficulties seem to always stand and be there right in front of you, never dissolving.

Millard said it boldly in his Facebook post:

"God is worthy long before any of those circumstances even showed up. In fact, what Christ has already done on the cross is probably the only thing we need to get through those circumstances. It's a foundation that was built long before those difficulties came to be. This song is a declaration to God that even if He went silent and never said another word, He's still worthy to be praised and that He's our greatest hope in the midst of the trial."

Those difficult circumstances can be diabetes, cancer, anxiety, depression, migraines, PTSD, stress ... they can be anything. God is so much more than any of those things, even if He doesn't fix them right away. He has created a firm foundation for us, and we know that He could save us even when we are standing in the fire. When we are standing in the worst imaginable place, we know that He can save us. We know that He can save us even when we don't feel like praising

---

9   Law, J. (2019). *MercyMe's Frontman Bart Millard Pens 'Even If' Song on Heartbreak Over Son's Chronic Illness.* Christianpost.com.

Him. He is the rock and the one who can truly make things happen, as well as make good come from the evil that finds its way into our lives.

Even if you fail the test, even if you get a job promotion. Even if you sin, even if you resist temptation. Even if, He is always there. He is always and forever worthy to be praised. He who has saved us from the darkness that threatens to succumb our hearts and minds. He is there.

Millard in this sense reminds me a lot of Job when thinking about how both he and Job had to persevere through a lot. They have their differences in situations, but they both had to persevere and trust God. By trusting God, Millard was able to create and produce an incredible song that inspires both himself and others, and Job was able to receive all of his fortune back.

All it takes is trusting God through the hard times and trials, because in the end He will bless you for your strength and perseverance. No matter your situation, He will move you through it. He worked with Job despite Job having anxiety issues, and He worked with Millard and his son as they moved through a hardship with a sickness.

As we go through our sufferings when our mental health flares up and acts out, regardless of whether it is a disorder or not, it is very easy for us to see the negative and fear that the absolute worst thing imaginable could happen. Fear not though, because God is one who is worthy of all praise, and He is the one who will pull us from our dark places. He will guide us through these waters.

Even if the diagnosis says the condition you fear the most, He will see you through. Even when you don't feel like swimming or treading through those deep blue waters, He will guide you and provide you with strength to get through those hardships. Even when things just look like they are falling around you, you will find your way, by God's grace.

No matter where you find yourself, God will make a way through.

My best friend Carlos Evans had the great God-given wisdom on what to do when you are in times of trouble: go to the Word. Carlos mentions how in the Bible you are able to see how other people have gone through the same struggles you have. It may look a little different, but there are similarities, and it is a comfort to realize that other people understand you.

Connecting this point to mental health, we can truly realize that by reading His Word and by praising Him, a lot of the things we suffer from will be relieved. Why we are feeling a certain way will likely become clearer. It brings a great sense of comfort to know that people in the Bible, such as Job, dealt with anxiety issues and that pressing worry. It makes us feel safe and secure to know these things, and that is what God promises us.

It shows us that people who are talked about in the Bible had struggles too. We see how in the entirety of the Book of Job he is dealing with struggles that are hectic and cause a lot of fear. We see in John 11:35 NIV[10] that "Jesus wept." All of the

10   Bible Gateway. (2019) *Bible Gateway Passage: John 11:35 New International Version [online]*

individuals in the Bible have their own respective struggles, in whatever way they may manifest. This point is essential for us to know as believers because we get so caught up in thinking every single person in the Bible is perfect. We see anxiety mentioned in the Bible. Doubt, fear, worry, and stress are all mentioned in the Bible.

This should give you confidence as well because no one on earth is truly perfect. Every single person you walk by has their own personal struggles or unspoken battles. It could be a thing from the past, it could be in the present, or sadly it could be something coming in the future. Even if we deal with these battles and struggles, such as mental health conditions or just things that life throws at us, we can rest assured and know that God is with us through it all.

Even if our lives are looking hectic and things don't make much sense, we are still called to trust Him that He will make a way for us. We are called to trust that no matter what the answer is, it will glorify Him and strengthen us both as humans but also in our walk with Him. Everything we deal with will all come full circle and the reason certain things happened will make sense.

Never forget that you are never alone, and that there are people and songs that you can relate to that will push you from your dark spots. Even if the answer looks foggy, trust Him. It will all be worth it, and this trust will produce strength that is needed to fight your fight with mental health disorders.

END OF CHAPTER TAKEAWAYS:

BIBLE VERSES:
- Job 3:20-23 NIV
- Daniel 3:17 NIV
- Job 42:12 NIV
- John 11:35 NIV

QUESTIONS FOR REFLECTION:
- Thinking about Job and his complexities, how does it feel for you to know that there is someone in the Bible who worked so hard and trusted God but still failed?
- How are you going to handle rejection and the "no's" as they come about?

ACTIONABLE TAKEAWAYS:
- Meditate and study the Book of Job.
- Write some quotes that motivate you for times in which you are dealing with stress, fear, or rejection.

PRAYER:
Hey God. I'm in a weird place in my life right now, because I have struggled with rejection and things just aren't going the way I expected them to. I pray that you will keep my heart, eyes, and mind open to your goodness and to the prosperity you promise, just like you promised for Job. Amen.

CHAPTER 4

WON'T STOP NOW

——

As we go through these trials and anxiety-inducing dilemmas, we find that it is very easy to become stuck in a rut. Meaning, we find that it is easy to just close and push away everything around us, even the joyous things, and drown in our misery. It is very simple for us to succumb to that numbness and it becomes a great challenge to pull ourselves out of that darkness and despair.

However, we are not called or made to drown. We are not called to drown even if we fall off the ship that is moving across the raging sea. We are called to continue to move forward and to prove to ourselves that we can win this war—the war that is raging, the war that is flaming. We are called to pull ourselves back onto the ship even if takes all of our might and strength. We are called by Christ to fight the good fight and call on Him to give us strength and to lead us across the raging oceans.

Deuteronomy 31:8 NIV: Lord himself goes before you and will be with you; he will never leave you nor forsake you. Do not be afraid; do not be discouraged.[11]

Despite dealing with the unknown and the hardships that develop, the Lord is always there next to us. He has seen the storm before us, and He knows exactly what will happen minute by minute. He knows when you will run to Him, when you will be annoyed with Him, and when you will cry out to Him in praise. He knows all, and He knows that fear and anxiety are crippling. He is not the kind of God who would wish that on anyone, and He wants us to trust in Him and to never fear during the hardships. He has already paved out the gravel dirt road, and has made our path straight and smooth. It is imperative that we cling to Him and trust Him, even when our soul isn't aflame and even when we are barely holding onto the side of the ship. He is working in the midst, always.

**

Many times, I have felt sluggish due to anxiety overwhelming my soul. I would feel it creeping up on me at the most inconvenient times and draining me both emotionally and physically. Honestly, it can be common to have a good few days and then feel the pressure—a noticeable shift that comes

11   Bible Gateway. (2019). Bible Gateway Passage: Deuteronomy 31:8 – New International Version. [online]

out of nowhere. We learn that this is in fact the Devil trying to sweep us away from the blessings our Lord has given us.

A friend of mine once said, "Satan can not create anything by himself, he has to steal what God has made for good and turn it for evil." This statement is vital in those periods of anxiety. It is so important to remember that there is still a purpose for us. It's also important to remember that these flare-ups and hard times do not dictate our relationship with Christ.

The best way to drown out what Satan is trying to speak to you is by finding the positives within the situation. It's important to remember that this too shall pass and that the truth of the situation will come out soon. As Deuteronomy 31:6 NIV[12] says, "Be strong and courageous. Do not fear or be in dread of them, for it is the Lord your God who goes with you. He will not leave you or forsake you." While it is easy to fear the future because of the knowledge that Satan changes good to evil, it is imperative that you cling to the Lord and know that He has an incredible future planned for you. Everything will all work out according to His plan. Don't stop trusting in His plan now.

It is important for us to stay grounded in our faith during these low points and to not allow the Devil to shift the flow and make us become entrapped in his lies. God has given us so many blessings, and Satan sees that goodness and he tries to attack those blessings to harm us greatly.

---

12 Bible Gateway. (2019). Bible Gateway Passage: Deuteronomy 31:6 – New International Version. [online]

Do not allow the Devil to cause you to change your beliefs. Do not succumb to the lies that he feeds you. You are still strong and wonderful no matter your past or present, and the Lord will continue to see you through your troubles. The Lord will still use you even when you are at your lows; He will still use you even in your brokenness. We are just called to keep fighting.

Psalm 147:3 NIV: He heals the brokenhearted and binds up their wounds.[13]

We won't stop now. This is a firm statement, but it is also a strong and powerful one with regard to staying strong in your good fight and not settling in the middle of a mess you're in. We are called to move forward and to not stop moving because the Lord will soon bind up our wounds, whether physical or mental.

It is easy to feel that you need to slow down or stop trusting the Lord, but don't stop. Don't stop moving, don't stop loving others, and don't stop being the child of God that you are. Even while we wait, it is important that we keep moving and living out our lives for Christ. It is essential to your faith journey that you continue to stay strong and that you continue to put your best foot forward. The circumstances may look

13   Bible Gateway. (2019). Bible Gateway Passage: Psalm 147:3 – New International Version. [online]

rough, but remember that you could be standing right on the edge of glory and joy. Always keep moving.

The Lord deserves all glory; thank Him for bringing you and pulling you through the incredibly intense and tough times. He brings us through the valleys; He pulls us out of the trenches; He is good. Think about that moment after you survive a struggle through something difficult and you feel ready for the next big thing. In the song "Won't Stop Now" by Elevation Worship, the line "I'm ready for whatever You want to do" resonates with me deeply. It shows how the Lord brings us through the hard times, and then we receive His grace and are ready to jump onto the next thing and grow that way.

Don't fear if you get stuck at a crossroads trying to figure out which direction to take. The Lord will make your path very clear for you. The Lord will show you a path of peace. He will allow you to grow, but He sometimes throws those little obstacles at us in order to mold us and shape our faith. Always trust in Him because He will do some pretty spectacular things in your life. While you're so focused on what is going to happen on the opposite end of that crossroad, the Lord could be calling you to focus on where you are in the present moment.

**

God's presence is an open door, and He is always welcoming and kind. He wants us to open our hearts and minds. He wants to give us wisdom that will inspire us to grow, and He wants to change our lives. The song "Won't Stop

Now" brings to mind a moment where someone has just accepted Jesus Christ into their life; by listening to this song you will likely see what I mean. It reminds me of how joyous a person is when they accept Jesus into their life, and when they begin to experience His holy presence. It is an amazing thing to feel this way. It also reminds me of the hunger, thirst, and ultimate need we have for our Savior. It is so deep within us, yet so present once we dig for it and pay attention to it.

We will reach a point of pure hunger for His grace. There is a certain point we get to in our walk with Christ where we simply get hungry. We have that urge, need, desire, and thirst for His grace and to know Him. Even when we feel that He is finished, we can trust that there will be so much more abundant grace to come.

The song "Won't Stop Now" by Elevation Worship is truly a fight song. This is a fight song that is meant to shake the rafters above in the church building. This is a fight song that is meant to allow the church—the body—to roar. This is a fight song that is meant to declare the Lord's goodness against the Devil's demise. The best is always on the way. It's time to scream that and to declare it straight into the Devil's face when evil crosses into our lane. Put the cross right in front of you, bear it, and know that the Lord will do good things, all because of our focus and trust in Him. As long as we put Him first and declare to the Heavens that His grace is not only sufficient but mighty, the best is coming. The best is always on the way, even when we are in the darkest low that we have ever experienced.

The Lord has promised. The Lord will deliver. The Lord has promised us that we will make it through, that we will see the victory and the promised land on the other side of this gaping hole. The Lord has promised a breakthrough. Due to faith, we have that ability to see a miracle and to know that it is on its way. It may take some time, or it could be right on the other side of that corner, but it is there. There's no way to stop it from happening—it will happen.

The Lord will provide, the Lord will deliver, and the Lord will continue to use you to build His mighty kingdom. Your breakthrough is on the way. Always trust that you will find it. It will come to you when it is time, but you will break through the glass. You will shatter it into pieces once you learn of the peace that Jesus has promised you. Your breakthrough is here. It is coming. It will be here. No matter when it comes, thank Jesus for it. Keep praying endlessly. The Lord is ready; you just have to trust Him.

Don't stop trusting in the Lord. Don't stop putting your best foot forward and trusting in Him, even during the most difficult circumstances. Declare to the Heavens that you won't stop now. No one can hold back a raging Lion. No one can hold back what the Lord has prepared for you. Don't stop, even when the wait gets to be too much or too hard. The wait will also continue to strengthen you and prepare you for what is to come.

Don't stop, even when your anxiety or depression is weighing on your shoulders. The Lord will carry you on His back to pull you through. Don't stop when you are in the middle of a crisis and you feel like you can't hear or find the Lord. In these situations, the Lord is carrying you. He is carrying you across those waters. Trust Him, and declare to Him that you won't stop now, or ever. Don't stop fighting, don't stop trying, and don't stop trusting. It will all be okay, and that I promise you.

You are not called to drown. You are called to swim, no matter how rocky the waves get.

END OF CHAPTER TAKEAWAYS:

BIBLE VERSES:
- Deuteronomy 31:8 NIV
- Deuteronomy 31:6 NIV
- Psalm 147:3 NIV

QUESTIONS FOR REFLECTION:
- When you listen to the song "Won't Stop Now" by Elevation Worship, what do you gather about the song itself? When you listen to it, do you feel determined?
- How does it feel to hold God's promises so close to your heart and to know not to quit fighting?
- What is a personal takeaway you have from this chapter?

ACTIONABLE TAKEAWAYS:
- Listen to fight songs, such as "Won't Stop Now." It's easy when we're experiencing hard times to only want to have "Sad Girl/Boy Hours," meaning we only listen to sad music. Use this as an opportunity to cry your tears and get your anger out, but to then get back up on your feet and listen to a fight song.

PRAYER:
Dear Lord, I am in a situation. I am stuck in a rut. I feel that I don't know if I should keep moving forward or stop. I am unsure of where to look next ... forward, back, down, up, around? Where do I go, Father? I ask you to direct my steps and show me the way. I am ready.

CHAPTER 5

WHY AM I ANXIOUS?

———

The golden question. The one we ask when we feel shards of anxiety piercing our skin like glass. The question that presses our minds deeply and makes us question the hair raising up on our arms. The one we ask when we just don't know exactly why we're feeling this way. The feeling of the unknown enveloping us.

I understand this. That feeling is exactly what sent me to get help at Clemson CAPS, the mental health service on Clemson University's campus, one Friday morning my freshman year in September 2018. I remember the night before I decided to go; I was sitting at my desk and I had no idea why I was anxious. I began feeling really weird and stressed about things, and I knew this wasn't right. My roommate, Hannah Fortune, was there, and I told her my dilemma.

I looked up the CAPS website and took a screening test to determine if this was something I should actually pay attention to. The results from that suggested that I have Generalized Anxiety Disorder (GAD). From that moment, I realized that I had an issue on my hands that was bigger than anything I could deal with on my own.

My first message to you is that it is imperative to seek help if it is common for you to feel anxious out of nowhere, generally down and depressed, or both of these things that can make you go from high to low in an instant. Before that night when I was just confused as to why I was anxious, I had already been feeling abnormally worked up and on edge about other things. That moment just sealed the deal on me going to seek help.

One day, I came across a sermon from Pastor Steven Furtick of Elevation Church out of Charlotte, North Carolina entitled "Why Am I Anxious?"[14] Furtick begins with relaying the message of David. He tells how David once viewed things from an external perspective and blamed his anxiety on outward things, but then one day he chose to flip the flow and take an inward perspective. He viewed this process as the internal versus external. This is a really important message, because I too sometimes will blame my anxiety on things that are happening externally. While this is valid because some things that happen externally do trigger our anxiety, we can still aim to control points of it within ourselves.

---

14 Elevation Church. *"Why Am I Anxious? | Bars & Battles | Pastor Steven Furtick"* Filmed [August 2017]. Youtube video, posted August 2017.

Psalm 139:23 NIV: Search me, God, and know my heart; test me and know my anxious thoughts![15]

This is David's plea that really shakes things up, in a good way. He is beginning to realize that it may not always be the external that causes anxiety, but rather the internal. As Furtick says, David was originally worrying about what the people around him were doing, and then suddenly just flipped the flow and asked God to "search [him]." He asked God to help him to search himself internally, rather than look to external events or circumstances. Tying into a later chapter of mine, Furtick makes the strong, powerful, and extremely true point (that I can attest to) that "nothing changes until I do."

It's easy to just go to therapy and say that you are making big gains in your mental health journey, but then walk out and not make the changes needed to better your mental health. It's easy for Christians, like my Uncle Harold says, to go to church every Sunday but to not live out the Word and truth for the full seven days of the week. It's easy to post about the grand changes you're making, without really following through. It's about staying true to your word and God's plan for you.

God wants us to make these changes, and He wants us to put in work to find out what works for us. He wants us to

---

15   Bible Gateway. (2019). *Bible Gateway Passage: Psalm 139:23 – New International Version.* [online]

make these changes and be able to answer the question "Why am I anxious?" honestly. Something external could have legitimately triggered you, such as a bad incident from which you suffer from PTSD. However, the trigger could also be internal—what you're filling your heart with.

Going back to Pastor Furtick's message, he pulled out his phone to demonstrate turning your phone off. Our phones fill up so much of our minds with clunky material that has no right to be there. We try to fill the voids in our lives with the worldly "perfection" or acceptance we get from having a certain number of likes on social media, the perfectly set filters on photos, and the acceptance from people who don't care about our hearts.

The seemingly perfect lives of other people take up space in our heart and cause us great distress if we feel like we aren't the exact same or doing more than them. It is very easy to get wrapped up in sentiments like, "Oh, he didn't text me back fast enough," or, "Oh, she was online five minutes ago and liked so and so's picture but didn't text me back." These moments can cause us stress and lead to social anxiety. Personally, I deal with the struggle of wondering why people aren't texting me back as fast I expected they would. This is not a healthy trait and I wholeheartedly accept that. However, it's up to you and me to flip that flow and decide what garners importance and should have a spot in our minds.

Psalm 139:24 NIV: See if there is any offensive way in me, and lead me in the way everlasting.[16]

Furtick makes the powerful comparison that while David likely didn't know much about neural pathways, which are factors in mental health disorders, it seemed like he did. We can deduce that when he says "offensive," he likely means different. He is asking God to lead him in a manner that is everlasting and powerful and will deliver him from these differences he may have. He begins to understand that this could be an internal thing he's dealing with ... one that comes from a biological standpoint.

That's a key factor for us when we think about our own mental health disorders: it is a biological thing. Christians can and do have mental health disorders. There once was such a stigma against that, and it was denied that Christians could even have these issues. Even David himself had clued in to the fact that there could be something wrong with the neural pathways in his brain. He doesn't complain about it but rather prays that God will deliver him from it and help him work through it.

According to WebMD,[17] researchers are taking note on how there are differences and abnormalities in terms of connections between nerve cells along various circuits

---

16   Bible Gateway. (2019). *Bible Gateway Passage: Psalm 139:24 – New International Version.* [online]

17   Goldberg, Joseph. "Mental Health: The Brain and Mental Illness." WebMD, WebMD, April 6 2019.

and pathways. These differences can lead to issues with the brain processing thoughts, which can result in abnormal moods, behaviors, and thoughts. WebMD also brings the opinions of several researchers to the table, as they believe that changes in the shape or size of various parts of the brain could be a factor in the development of mental health disorders.

Going back to Pastor Furtick's sermon on David and the neurological pathways, I think that he got it right. Mental health disorders are caused by actual biological issues that could present themselves due to abnormal nerve cells or genetics. Mental health disorders could present themselves due to dealing with substance abuse, an abusive person in your life (whether in childhood or the present day), or trauma in general, amongst many other incidents. Having these disorders is not a choice.

I did not wake up one day and say, "Hey God, give me anxiety!" Why on earth would I do something of the sort? My point is that no one ever asks for pain or for suffering. No one asks to constantly ask and wonder the answer of the question, "Why am I anxious?" That's just not real. No one asks for things to happen that aren't ideal, but we all know that they will strengthen us.

That's the kind of tactic we should all take on this. When we have that dreaded question come to mind, "Why am I anxious?" we can fall back and remember that while the cause can be external, it definitely can be internal, too. It's important to remember what we're filling our hearts and minds with, and to also remember that something could be a little funky neurologically—and that part can be treated with medication.

> Isaiah 41:10 NIV: So do not fear, for I am with you;
> do not be dismayed, for I am your God.
> I will strengthen you and help you;
> I will uphold you with my righteous right hand.[18]

This verse from Isaiah really has a special place in my heart because it is a verse that has personally pushed me through so much, such as through the times in my college career when I had no idea what was going on. God is right there with us, not just in the times of nerves and jitters, but also in the highs. No biological difference outweighs His presence. He will uphold you with His righteous right hand, even when you are trembling due to the doubt and fear that weighs heavy on your heart.

Rather than trust filling our hearts and minds, they are filled with fear and worry: fear that we aren't good enough, worry that we will never understand our true calling, and similar feelings replace that trust. We are called to know that God has His watchful eye on us at all times. While it is understandable to feel unsettled because a mental health disorder

---

18   Bible Gateway. (2019). *Bible Gateway Passage: Isaiah 41:10 – New International Version* [online]

is a legitimate disorder that causes some physical issues, it is no match for our God. The perturbed feelings and the times when you are ridden with anxiety are no match for the closeness to our God, and no match for the peace He has for you. This is imperative to learn now, but Chapter 10, Locations, will further explain this point.

The final point I will make here is from Pastor Furtick; he asked this great rhetorical question:

Why am I anxious if He has numbered the hairs on my head?

He knows you for exactly who you are. You are His child, His loved one. He loves you in an unimaginable capacity, and He molded you to be who you are. This mental health disorder you may struggle with does not define you. It is simply what He has placed in your life that will allow you to grow closer in your faith and find time to worship Him and cling to Him. He does all things for good.

God knows all of us. He sees the 43.8 million people[19] who suffer from mental disorders every year. He sees all 7.7 billion of us working toward our goals, and He sees everyone jumping for joy in their victories and managing their wounds. He sees us. He knows us, and He has promises for all of us.

Cling to his white robe. Cling to Him when you are happy. Cling to Him when you are sad. Cling to Him when you are anxious. Cling to Him when you are angry, excited, or any

---

19   "5 Surprising Mental Health Statistics." Mental Health First Aid, February 6, 2019.

other emotion. He will always be right there next to you. He knows you, and He is with you. Never forget His goodness, and never forget all He has done for you, because it is incredible. There are so many more incredible things to come.

Take it step by step, stay consistent in prayer and fellowship, and remain constant in worship. He has saved you from your darkest nights and has spoken through Pastor Furtick and me to bring you this message of truth. You will make it through; don't stop now.

END OF CHAPTER TAKEAWAYS:

BIBLE VERSES:
- Psalm 139:23 NIV
- Psalm 139:24 NIV
- Isaiah 41:10 NIV

QUESTIONS FOR REFLECTION:
- When you think about your personal struggles in life, do you feel equipped to fight them? How so?
- How has God worked through the season you are in? Whether that season be a low or high, how has He worked?

ACTIONABLE TAKEAWAYS:
- Write out each way He has worked in your life within the past day, then week, then month, then year, and so on.
- If you begin to have a case of the "what if's" or "Why am I anxious/depressed/fearful/doubtful/etc." write down those questions and then try to answer them to the best of your ability.

PRAYER:
Heavenly Father, I stand before you tonight in a season of the unknowns. This season is promising, although I have no idea what it is completely in store for me. Through this season of unknowns and everything that comes with that, I pray that you will keep me grounded in your love and grace and allow me to cling to your robe throughout it all. You are so good to me. Amen.

CHAPTER 6

THE HOPE CYCLE

———

If you think about it long and hard, there truly is a cycle of hope. What I mean by this is that sometimes we are at the peak of hope—we are living out our lives with hope, joy, and promise. Then, something happens, bad stuff hits the fan, and we are left suffering. Our hope is much lower during this point, and this causes a good deal of anxiety and disappointment within us. Then, we have to learn to "fight," stay strong throughout the trial, and persevere through our battles. We decide and learn that we can't let it win; we have to prevail. Eventually, we realize that these so-called struggles really aren't as big as we believed they were, and our character begins to build.

Part of the message of Holly Furtick, from Elevation Church, is called "The Hope Cycle.[20]" Holly makes a great mention about how this hope cycle is one that never ceases.

———

20 Elevation Church. "The Hope Cycle | Holly Furtick" YouTube video, posted May 2019.

This cycle is something that we go through all of the time, whether we truly realize it or not. We are able to put this into words now, and we are able to visualize the very thing we go through that has been so misunderstood. This is incredibly important for us as believers and sufferers to realize that this is a very structured ordeal we go through.

Once we accept this structure, we are then able to identify and become more aware of all of these things as they begin to unfold. Holly does an incredible job of explaining this hope cycle, and it hit me pretty hard because all I could think about was my anxiety.

Personally, hearing this sermon provided a major sense of relief because this is something that everyone experiences. Even if you don't personally suffer from an anxiety disorder or any other mental disorder, to know that there is a consistent cycle of hope that allows us to grow is incredible. The passage below is proof that God will not, and never will, leave us hanging, no matter what comes our way. No matter the sleepless and tearful nights when we are so upset about our present situation, or the times when we question everything, faith included. Our God can't be scared away. He has this incredible promise of hope that will always win.

Romans 5:3-4 NIV: Not only so, but we also glory in our sufferings, because we know that suffering produces perseverance; perseverance, character; and character, hope.[21]

First things first, what hit me hard is just how exact this Bible verse is when we visualize the physical hope cycle. Holly pulls this visual of a hope cycle from Romans 5:3-4. In this passage, we learn about how God can use you and will build you during your trials. The bad will always end with the good, and that is proven through this passage. This is truly a chain reaction that happens as spoken in Romans. We learn how God allows these sufferings to happen, just like He allows the anxiety and depression we may experience, because He knows in the end that these things will build endurance and character.

Furthermore, the hope that is talked about in Romans 5 is a special hope, as Holly Furtick noted in her sermon. This is different from the generic hope, such as hoping that you

---

21 Bible Gateway. (2019). Bible Gateway Passage: Romans 5:3-4 – New International Version [online]

will get over your sickness. Rather, this is a hope that is put specifically in God. This type of hope, the special hope, is truly a hope in God. This isn't a hope that explicitly says what we believe; rather, it is an intrinsic hope that we know that God will work in whatever way He chooses. Essentially, as Holly says it: "We are operating out of the assumption that God is working all of the things for good." This is displayed through the hope cycle visual that Holly shared.

The visual starts with sufferings, then as you suffer you learn to persevere. As you persevere, it builds character. As you build character and your faith in God begins to grow stronger, you will build hope. It is an endless chain reaction that occurs in everyone's lives. For example, as Holly mentions, are you feeling like you are putting one foot in front of the other but having no idea where you are going? That counts as perseverance.

Continue to walk the walk, take up your cross, and follow God. Every single step will build perseverance. As you build this perseverance you will grow as a person in many ways. You will become more relaxed in character because you will know that this is all part of a cycle, and you will grow in character in terms of being a Christian.

These present-day sufferings truly are not meant to last forever. They are meant for you to learn to take the high road and allow God to work through you. Whether that means getting up a little earlier just to save time so you don't worry about being late to work, or because you feel God stirring your heart to get out of bed and do the dishes. Whatever that is, act on it because it will build that endurance within you.

It will allow your heart to get stronger and your mind to get faster. You will then begin to build character because you will have the drive and motivation to do these things again when you realize that they help you in the end.

While it truly is an uncomfortable situation to deal with the hard and painful things, facing them will produce strength in the end. These things that God is allowing you to go through are things He is pushing you to grow through. The anxiety that you're feeling will produce perseverance to teach you how to push through the anxious times and still work on your homework assignments or other obligations. The depression that you're going through will allow your character to build because as time goes on, you will become stronger and move toward being more optimistic in your day-to-day life.

All of these things you go through will, in the end, produce hope. Hope is such a powerful, God-given thing.

1 Peter 5:10 NIV[22]: And the God of all grace, who called you to his eternal glory in Christ, after you have suffered a little while, will himself restore you and make you strong, firm, and steadfast.

---

22 Bible Gateway. (2019). *Bible Gateway Passage: 1 Peter 5:10 – New International Version* [online]

This verse from 1 Peter should give you hope in this crazy life we live. Restoration and growth are ultimately found in hope. In those times when your sink is full of dirty dishes, He will restore you and enable you to have hope that you will be able to clean them. He will strengthen you when you are in the midst of a relapse. He calls you by name, and He knows you. He knows your heart.

This hope cycle is clear and defined, just like the Book of Romans states, and just as Holly Furtick noted. It's up to us to let go of our present-day struggles and hand them to God to work and grow through what we are facing. It's up to us to chase after perseverance and still prevail even after a long day's work. It's up to us to allow God to push us to move and get out of our comfort zone, wherever that may be, and do the things that are hard for us. One day, they will not be so hard for us because we will have built that character and endurance to move through these problems.

That's one of the clear reasons that my anxiety has lost the stronghold it once had on me. I have learned that it is a cycle. I try to consistently remember that any suffering truly won't last forever, and that so many amazing and powerful things will come. Let's be real: it is hard to persevere when you are ridden with anxiety. But I have seen how persevering and aiming to do my best has enabled me to be stronger and to more easily endure these moments. Granted, sometimes it does feel like I am riding waves that never settle, but I always know I will come out safe on the other side with more strength than I had before. It's not easy to deal with these things, but it is important to allow yourself to feel these things when they happen.

That can be a terrifying thought to have, to completely let go and allow yourself to feel that anxiety that's crashing over you and roaring in your mind, but it will allow for strength and perseverance. Everything will work out and you'll be in a much better spot than before. It will allow for your character to build and for your hope to grow stronger and stronger, so strong that you'll begin to naturally have hope even in the darkest and hardest of times.

END OF CHAPTER TAKEAWAYS:

BIBLE VERSES:
- Romans 5:3-4 NIV
- 1 Peter 5:10 NIV

QUESTIONS FOR REFLECTION:
- What part of the hope cycle do you feel you belong in, presently?
- How are you witnessing God working through your life in the midst of your location in the hope cycle?
- How do you feel knowing that there is such thing as a hope cycle?

ACTIONABLE TAKEAWAYS:
- Draw the Hope Cycle on a sticky note or on a piece of paper and hang it wherever you need to.
- Take a photo of this cycle and put it somewhere on your laptop or phone that is easily accessible.
- Reflect on the past locations you have been in on the hope cycle and envision how your present-day situation is helping you.

PRAYER:
Heavenly Father, I know You are good. I know You have a lot in store for my life despite my going through the present-day suffering or struggle as I continue to climb and grow. I am praying that you will give me the grace and mindset I need to achieve this goal. I know that You are mighty and powerful, so I am praying that You will allow me to move through this process as diligently and with as much strength as possible. Amen.

CHAPTER 7

THE TRENCH

———

Do you ever feel like you are falling down an invisible hole as a result of stress, anxiety, depression, or something else? Do you feel like you're slipping so much, and you just aren't quite sure how you will pull yourself back onto your feet? Have you ever felt that sturdy ship rumble and shake just a little more than from a normal wave? You are not alone, and this is totally normal.

Here's a story. One night, I was at the performing arts building on campus for the club dance classes I took. During a break between two classes, I felt my anxiety climbing. I primarily got anxious because of doubt and worry about my grades, which were not even bad to begin with. I felt myself sliding down a trench. However, right before I got too far down, I felt the Lord and I knew He was there. I mentally reached for Him to pull me out by praying to Him right then and there. I felt some peace but still felt a little shaky mentally.

That night when I got back, I remembered what Mary Ropp, my sweet sister from Sigma Alpha Omega, had told me just days before that sometimes we don't need rest as in sleep, but we do need to rest in other ways, as well. It took me until that night to realize what that meant. I decided to just hop in bed and take it easy by talking to God and praising Him for seeing me through that storm. I talked to Him about everything and how thankful I was in that moment.

I found the ultimate resolution: that I had gone through all of the anxiety-ridden and doubtful hard times that previous semester JUST to get to that moment—the moment when I realized it all had strengthened me and brought me this far. That the Lord did not just set me out and let me loose in the wild, or let me go down the trench, but that He was with me all along even when I felt as though He wasn't.

I also proclaimed that I was free. At this moment, I felt the presence of the Holy Spirit in a way I hadn't felt ever before. It was powerful and I knew I had won, and He released me from my chains fully. THE LORD AND I DEFEATED ANXIETY. This moment was an extremely powerful one. To this day, I look back on that moment and remember that anxiety does not have that stronghold on my life anymore. It is a mental health condition that, while I still deal with it daily in some way or another, doesn't have its hold on me like it once did.

Matthew 11:28 NIV: Come to me, all you who are weary and burdened, and I will give you rest.[23]

23   Bible Gateway. (2019). Bible Gateway Passage: Matthew 11:28 – New International Version [online]

I decided, after talking to God, to listen to some music. I took the tactical approach to listen to calming music, but that wasn't enough. Hillsong's "Remembrance" and Elevation Church's "Here Again" and "Do It Again (live acoustic)" was better for the situation. In that moment, hearing the first chords of "Remembrance," I felt like I needed to do MORE, because just listening to the songs while lying in the dark in my dorm room still was not enough. The Lord wanted MORE and I was starving.

At 11:03 p.m. I was singing by myself in my dorm room bed, just in awe of His goodness. Looking back on it, it makes me laugh, because I bet if anyone had walked by outside, they would have been confused. But in all seriousness, it was a very emotional and powerful moment that I experienced. I was in awe of how good He is and how good He continues to be. The Lord will always deliver us from our trials and from our burdens, and He will set us free. I defeated anxiety. Time and time again I have defeated anxiety. I haven't given up yet, and I do not plan on it.

When I feel anxious, I have learned the best way to fight is to be still and give it to the Lord. The Lord will fight your battles. It is a hard thing to give up because you feel so convinced that you can handle these battles yourself, but in reality, my friend, sometimes you just can't. I now always give it to the Lord. I may wrestle with the thoughts for a little while, but I ultimately push myself to pray and give them to the Lord. It is the best way to heal.

In this moment, I was also reminded of how important it is to accept your feelings rather than fight them away or push them to the back of your mind. That is a dangerous game, friends. It is important to embrace these emotions and accept them, as hard as that is, and give them to the Lord. Once you give them to the Lord, you can count on Him to grab your hands and pull you up out of that trench.

You do not deserve to be trapped in a trench. You deserve to be free and to let the Lord do the unimaginable. Everything that you have gone through up to this point in your life has prepared you for this moment. If you are struggling, this is your time to understand how the Lord is telling you that it is time to let your battles be His and to be still. It is time for you to allow the Lord to grab your hands and pull you up and out of that trench. This is your moment, and this is your time to be safe. Trust the Lord, and He will always deliver. Just like always.

END OF CHAPTER TAKEAWAYS:

BIBLE VERSE:
- Matthew 11:28 NIV

QUESTIONS FOR REFLECTION:
- When you feel like you are in the deep end, like you made a hefty mistake or something less than ideal happened in your life, what do you do first?
- How do you combat those feelings when you are submerged in the deep end, or the trench?

ACTIONABLE TAKEAWAYS:

- Read and memorize Matthew 11:28. It is incredible to remember this Bible verse and immediately feel peace.
- On a sheet, with Matthew 11:28 in the center, write things you can personally do when you need to rest and when you need to experience peace. Look back on this sheet when you are facing a hard time.

PRAYER:

Heavenly Father, I am truly in awe of your goodness and of how You are able to pull us up out of the grave and bring us to life. I am thankful that you have pulled me from the trench, and I pray that you will continue to do so now. Amen.

CHAPTER 8

THE GOOD FIGHT

———

When you picture a "good fight," you probably picture a wrestling match or something of that nature, in which people fight it out and one is declared the winner. You may picture someone standing on a pasture holding a white flag in the air symbolizing their surrender and the end of a battle. Or you may picture maybe the end of a basketball game when all of the players, coaches, and team personnel line up together and shake hands to say "good game." What does this look like when it comes to our struggles and anxieties though?

The phrase "good fight" went through my head so many times when I was dealing with pressure, anxiety, or stressful times. It was during these times I would somehow remember that this is a "good fight," even though it feels anything but good. The phrase "good fight" is actually found in the Bible, and we will look at that more closely later in this chapter.

What I mean is despite feeling like you are being punched in the gut while your mind is on fire, it still can be a positive thing to have struggles because they strengthen you. You can either look at these issues in life negatively or positively. It is important to look at them in as strong and positive of a light as you possibly can. Me calling it a good fight does not mean that it is good to be in mental pain or dealing with an internal battle. However, after going through it so much, it develops into a negative ordeal with a silver lining; that silver lining is that you are developing the strength you need to grow.

At times in life, it appears that a million things are all going wrong at once. As humans, it is easier to focus on the negative aspects of our situations rather than on the potential blessings. Hold fast to God's word. Once the storm has passed, you will rejoice once again. While the storm is active, rejoice then too.

You are alive and you are ABUNDANTLY loved, even if the world tells you otherwise. Do not listen to what the world says; listen to what our mighty Savior says. The Devil works hard when he sees how God is working in your life. Fear not and do not be shaken.

The Lord would never put you in a situation that would cause you to deteriorate. Every single situation will allow you to grow stronger with the Lord, and it will continue to allow you to grow in your faith. The Lord designs these "good fights" to pull you closer to Him and to allow your faith and mindset to grow.

**

When you're dealing with trials or in the midst of a dark place, it is very easy to think about the negative. In fact, it's pretty much a given that it'll happen at some point in time, and that's okay. Just don't let the Devil pull you down into a trench, and don't believe his lies. That is very dangerous ground to walk on and you must instead focus your mind on Christ to the best of your ability when you're under a mental or physical attack. It is much easier said than done, but after a lot of work and perseverance it will become second nature to do so.

The Lord will guide you through those waters. He will be there alongside you during your good fight, and He will bring His grace and glory to the table. You will find that peace, and you and your faith will grow tremendously. Never forget that there will be a silver lining and a happy ending to the hard time with which you are dealing. In order to make those hard times just a little bit easier, you need to switch your mindset. As said in 2 Timothy 4:7-8 NIV, it is imperative to keep fighting that good fight because you will earn the greatest reward imaginable on the day you meet Jesus.

2 Timothy 4:7-8 NIV: I have fought the good fight, I have finished the race, I have kept the faith. Now there is in store for me the crown of righteousness, which the Lord, the righteous Judge, will award to me on that day—and not only to me, but also to all who have longed for his appearing.[24]

24 Bible Gateway. (2019). Bible Gateway Passage: 2 Timothy 4:7-8 – New International Version [online]

One time I heard Pastor Steven Furtick from Elevation Church speak about "flipping the flow" and what that means. Flipping the flow essentially means to flip your thoughts from the dark ones and try to shine some light on the situation. After I heard this message, learning to flip the flow truly changed my life and helped my personal fight with anxiety so much. It is an incredible tool and it allows you to let the Lord in even when you are facing the hardest of circumstances.

One easy way to switch your mindset and flip the flow is by creating a gratitude journal or by just writing out your happy thoughts about things that are going right in your life. Make time each day to write about what you are thankful for, and find the good in every single tough situation. This is essential to do, but one of the most important pieces of the puzzle is to thank God for these things. Pray with gratitude and tell God everything for which you are thankful.

During this talk Furtick said, "Don't deal with on the surface what God wants to deal with at the root."[25] That's a pretty strong quote, and it can be a little bit hard to understand what it means. When I hear this quote, it brings me directly back to our topic of the good fight.

What makes these fights good is that when God is allowing things to stir you at the surface, He really is trying to provoke something within, at the root, and allow for that change to occur. This is a complex, deep, and extraordinary

---

25 *Flip It | Flip the Flow | Pastor Steven Furtick*. (2019). [video] Directed by S. Furtick. Elevation Church: Elevation Church.

way to think about how God is truly working in your life. Sometimes we feel so stuck in the mud, as though we can't accomplish anything more. When that happens, allow the Lord to work within you and drive these surface issues to change you within.

Finally, Pastor Steven Furtick shared another powerful tool: "When you know where your calling comes from, you can be confident in how your battle will turn out." Boom. There it is, y'all. That is the golden statement for this chapter.

We are called by the Lord to be truly confident in Him and to know that, while difficult and nerve-racking, our battles will end up okay, and we will end up stronger than we were before. In order to reach your calling, you will have to go through some rocky events. You will have to suffer from things and sometimes face a test in faith. All of this is totally normal, so allow it to happen, because in the end this good fight will be something you grow thankful for. This good fight will blossom and grow into a thing of true beauty, and you will receive your calling and His grace like rain.

Don't stop believing and always trust in His plan. No matter how far down you are, you can always come back up. Even if you feel like you can't come back up on your own, the Lord will grab you and pull you up. Even if you feel like crawling, keep fighting. Keep fighting and trusting His plan, and trust that He will see you through and create something amazing. When you get down, pray, ask for help, and just look anywhere but down. Set your focus on the things above, the things that are promising and happy.

Psalm 108:13 NIV: With God we will gain the victory, and He will trample down our enemies.[26]

In Him, the good fight will always end well. It may end with a slightly different outcome than we had hoped for, but it will all line up and make sense with His perfect plan one day.

Never fear the rocky waves or the people threatening to throw you off the ship into the strong currents. The Lord will trample our enemies and pave a safe and protective way for you to grow. He never leaves and He never forsakes. Keep your thoughts above and keep them focused on your safe place—the Lord's presence. Nothing can compare to the goodness He provides, so reside in that hope.

END OF CHAPTER TAKEAWAYS:

BIBLE VERSES:
- 2 Timothy 4:7-8 NIV
- Psalm 108:13 NIV

QUESTIONS FOR REFLECTION:
- Think of a time you unknowingly fought a good fight. How did that turn out? Are you still in one today? What will you do to progress through your current or next good fight?

---

26 Bible Gateway. (2019). Bible Gateway Passage: Psalm 108:13 – New International Version [online]

- How, in your opinion, can God use you through your good fight?

ACTIONABLE TAKEAWAYS:
- Create a gratitude journal as a means to notice your blessings in present-day situations.
- Stay in prayer and stay humble. Stay grateful, and challenge yourself daily to find one good thing, or more, that has happened. Psychological studies prove that doing so helps those who are consistently negative, or those who struggle to find the good in life.
- Place sticky notes around your room with little drawings or sayings from memorable times with your friends and family. My best friend, Kylee Trangmar, did this in her freshman year dorm and it was such a cute and memorable reminder of times before.

PRAYER:
Heavenly Father, today my heart is open to you. I am grateful and thankful for all you have done and all you continue to do. I am grateful for the mountains you have moved, the oceans you have calmed, and the paths you have shifted. I am grateful for all that you do, and I am thankful for the promises I know you have in store for me. Amen.

CHAPTER 9

ALL IN, ALL THE TIME

—

Proverbs 21:31 NIV: The horse is made ready
for the day of battle,
but victory rests with the Lord.[27]

The final seconds are on the clock of the 2016 College Football National Championship. The crowd is roaring, people are screaming, fans are about to come over the gates. There are three seconds on the clock. Deshaun Watson, quarterback, passes to Hunter Renfrow, wide receiver. The crowd goes nuts. The score is 34-31. An extra point is scored, and the final score of the "natty" is 35-31.

Dabo Swinney, head football coach of the legendary Clemson Football Program, said, "At the top of the mountain, that

---

27 Bible Gateway. (2019). Bible Gateway Passage: Proverbs 21:31 – New International Version [online]

Clemson flag is flying."[28] Nothing felt more vivid or true than this.

Looking back at footage from that football game, I am reminded of something that got my Tigers to the trophy: perseverance. They fought their hearts out, and they kept their optimism and faith at the highest it could be. They kept their priorities straight through practices, workouts, games, meetings, etc.; they all held it together.

That is how we are called to live as Christians. We are called to stay strong and cling to God, and to trust Him as we climb these mountains that so commonly rise right in front of us. We are called to not let the sharpness and jadedness of the journey throw us off course. We are called to pray and to not give up. In the midst of our hardships, we are still called to serve and love others. My dear friend Mary Ropp from Sigma Alpha Omega described serving as an essential way that she keeps her mental health in check. It keeps her heart and mind happy, and it is so good to do good unto others.

Galatians 6:9 NIV: Let us not become weary in doing good, for at the proper time we will reap a harvest if we do not give up.[29]

28 Dabo Swinney, Clemson Football. (2017). Twitter.
29 Bible Gateway. (2019). Bible Gateway Passage: Galatians 6:9 – New International Version [online]

As we go through trials and doubts, harm and pain, we have to realize that the Lord will deliver us and allow us to grow through these situations and circumstances. He will allow us to receive all of the promises and blessings that He has promised for us and that He has had in mind for us. He sees us as we grow, He sees us as we push through the trials that are staring us in the face. He sees how we interact when we are staring the Devil in the eye, and He gives grace upon grace when He sees our compassion for others.

God sees Dabo's compassion for his players, for his coaching staff, for his family, and for the Clemson family and nation. We see how Dabo does good for others, and we see how he and his wife are monumental in the fight against breast cancer. We see how they carry their cross and do good unto others. We see how they walk, and we see how they walk in the name of Jesus. Dabo is "all in, all the time" no matter if he is on the football field or in a Subway serving and making subs for members of the community.

It's about giving back. It's about having your heart set on things above, not the worldly things. It would be so easy for Dabo to focus solely on the gold shine that bounces off of the coveted National Championship trophy. It could be so easy for his coaching staff to be wrapped up in the rankings that come out on Sunday and Monday. But instead, they choose daily to focus on their team. They focus on the well-being of the team, the plays being made in practice, and the hearts that they lead.

As Coach Swinney said in the post-game team meeting of the 2016 national championship, that Clemson flag is definitely flying. The team that was doubted, the team that people said could not get there, did. They won that battle, and they won it at the last second.

And that, my friends, is what matters. It does not matter what the timeline looks like for your faith walk, for your battle against your mental health disorder, for how many times you've worked out. What matters is having perseverance and a drive to succeed in order to rise against the odds in the moments you never saw coming. At the end of the day, I know it is a special thing to look back after you won a war and built some dynasty, but it matters only on the buildup and the brick-by-brick scenario.

We can't expect God to just come into our life and fix everything all at once and give us our big trophy right away. However, we CAN expect God to give us the strength and dignity to get through various things that come our way, and to help us grow through the ashes and weeds, through the low-scoring games and the failed plays.

James 1:12 NIV: Blessed is the one who perseveres under trial because, having stood the test, that person will receive the crown of life that the Lord has promised to those who love him.[30]

---

30 Bible Gateway. (2019). Bible Gateway Passage: James 1:2 – New International Version [online]

I remember watching Clemson football for years before the team was on top of the rankings, as they are now. I remember seeing them slowly get stronger, better, and more well developed. I remember seeing this, and I remember being up at midnight with my family watching my Tigers win the national championship. I cried tears of joy in that moment, and now, a few years later, I can reexamine it from the angle of perseverance. Still, I'm emotional because that moment was so amazing.

The growth is what matters. It took years, seasons, hours of training, and a lot of work for the Tigers to get to the top of the leader board. It just takes time. Everything that is worthwhile takes time. Everything will pay off; all of your hard work, determination, faith, drive, and motivation will pay off. All of the tears and anger you may experience will pay off. Everything will work out perfectly, and the Lord will continue to provide for you.

One thing about Dabo Swinney that everyone is sure to notice is that he lives out his faith every day and he loves his team, his Clemson family, and his family. He is such an inspiration to me because of how he continues to live out his life for Christ no matter what people say online or in person during interviews with him.

During one interview with Sports Spectrum, Dabo was asked about his faith. "It's hard to survive and thrive in this world if you don't have a spiritual foundation," he said. "For me, God has always, in my relationship with Christ, has given me hope and peace … If there's hope in the future, there's power in the present to deal with whatever mess you're dealing with in your life, [and] what Christ did for me, it gave me a hope and a belief beyond my circumstances."[31]

What Dabo said during that interview resonates deeply with me, because it really is difficult to survive in the world we live in today if you don't have some sort of a spiritual faith. Between the stress that comes from everything that pops into your life to the things that we read in tabloids and social media, it is so important that you have a relationship with Christ to get you through it all. There are so many things in life that will threaten to change you and cause you to worry about yourself, but it is so important to have that relationship with Christ to know the difference between reality and the lies. Dabo speaks some serious truth here about how the Lord will give you that peace and hope to deal with whatever comes up, and in whatever situation—no matter how messy it is—you are dealing with in life.

To see how Dabo gives all of the glory to the Lord after a game, no matter win or lose, is truly inspirational, and I feel like we all could learn something from that. It is so easy to be wrapped up in the negative stuff that we deal with, and to not thank the Lord for what He has done. It is imperative for our walk with Christ and everything in our lives that we try to find the bright side of the things from which we suffer. Win or lose, the Lord will still love you; just know that the best victory you could possibly experience is to know the Lord and to know that He is good and He has saved you.

---

31 "Clemson Coach Dabo Swinney: Jesus Helps Me 'Survive and Thrive'." 2019. Sports Spectrum. October 29, 2019.

Finally, in an interview following the 2018 National Championship win against Alabama, Dabo said, "It is simply the grace of the Lord to allow us to experience something like this." To see the Tigers win the game in such an incredible fashion, overcome all of the adversity news outlets had thrown at them, and keep such a strong winning streak was nothing but God's grace. To see your name in flashing lights at the stadium and to hear the roar of your fans as you come back to Clemson, South Carolina has to be such an incredible opportunity. There are some things that seem so grand and large and unbelievable, but as mentioned before, God can do the impossible and the unimaginable.

That is how I felt when I would defy the odds and defeat my anxiety. I would realize that the only answer for this comes by the grace of God. It comes from persevering and building character, as mentioned in the Hope Cycle. It's about caring for your crew and for helping them win the game that they always dreamed of winning, like Dabo did. Finally, like my sister Elizabeth Radecki said in response to being involved in numerous activities—such as her high school yearbook team, student council, orchestra, strings, and AP classes—it is about being "all in" for Jesus. It is important to her that she is all in for Jesus and trusts Him throughout the craziness and busyness that comes from being involved in so much. It is about focusing on and being "all in" for everything she does, about pouring into everything she does. Dabo is all in for his team, Elizabeth is all in for her obligations, and Jesus is all in for YOU.

He is all in for you. The most high, the most beautiful name there is, is 100 percent all in for you. He knows you by name;

He knows exactly what will happen. He has given us this promise, the promise that we will be freed from all of the bad things that come our way. The promise that our anxiety will not win. The promise that our depression will not win. The promise that He is all in to help us through our struggles and see our way to a victory.

Our victory may not always include a shiny trophy, but it will include receiving the promise and truth that God has ensured for us. It will include the truth that no matter how stressed we become, we will find a way out. We will find a way to win our wars that rage within our hearts and minds. God has promised us eternal life, and that is the ultimate victory within it all.

Jesus is all in for us. That day He was nailed to the cross, He was all in for us. He still is all in for us. He knew us by name then, He knew what sins we would commit thousands of years later. He knew our hearts. He loved us then, just like He does now. He is all in for you.

When the depression lies to you and tells you that you are not worthy, that you are alone and that you are not loved, look to the cross. Look at what happened that dark day on the cross. Think about the message I am sharing with you about how Jesus is all in for us, all the time.

Be all in for Him. Be all in for your team, your classmates, and your family. Be all in for your obligations and for the things that stack up on top of each other. Pour into one another, but also pour into yourself. Remember that Jesus is always all in, so therefore we should be too as we are called to live like Jesus.

END OF CHAPTER TAKEAWAYS:

BIBLE VERSES:

- Proverbs 21:31 NIV
- Galatians 6:9 NIV
- James 1:12 NIV

QUESTIONS FOR REFLECTION:

- When you think about the triumph that Clemson had in the national championship (regardless of whether or not you are a Clemson Tigers fan) and other general triumphs you have in day-to-day life, how can you see God working?
- Was there any particular triumph or big win in your life where you saw God's hands all over it? What was that like for you?

ACTIONABLE TAKEAWAYS:

- When you are in a season of doubt, write down or think about those amazing triumphs you have had. Use this as a time of reflection to consider that, while life may look different now, God still has incredible promises for you in store.
- Keep Bible verses that have pushed you during your hard moments, and those verses that have helped you in the past, handy.

- Keep a bullet journal or just a journal of some form, depending on your preference, to keep all of your memories in there.

PRAYER:

Hey God, I want to be all in. Not just in the little moments or the things that don't have as long of an impact, but in all things. Father, I need the strength to stay focused and driven even when things aren't clear and the ground is shaky. I need the courage to continue on and stay focused, even when I feel like I am a lost cause or that there isn't any hope for my situation. Amen.

CHAPTER 10

LOCATIONS

———

Everyone probably shares their location via cell phone with someone. It could be a friend, family member, significant other, you name it, you probably have done it. It is common in this day and age to share these locations with one another for safety reasons and just to keep up with one another in case you need to get in touch with someone.

Sharing these locations raises some provoking thoughts. One night I was just sitting in my room, looking at this quote:

"Anxiety shows that we are too close to the world, and too far from God."

—JOHN PIPER.

Too far from God. Whoa! That is extremely powerful, and it shows me how our location is imperative in our walk with Christ. This quote really stuck with me in the idea that our walk with Christ is all based on location. Anxiety is one of those concepts that deals with location, whether we really realize it or not.

We're too close to the world. What does this even mean? Maybe we're too close to worldly things: the prizes, the fame, the money, the recognition. Maybe we're too close to other worldly things like anxiety, depression, stress, anger, etc. What it means for something to be worldly is that it is not of God.

When things are not of God and of His Holy Spirit, we begin to grow restless in a different sort of way. What do I mean by this? I mean that we grow restless in that we experience this suffering, we experience this worry and doubt, but why? It's because we are not close to Him in that moment.

Think about it like this. All of those moments when you are suffering, and your head is rumbling with the lies and you feel like you are about to be pulled under into those roaring waves—where is God? Where is He in your focus?

Really, and I experience this too, He probably isn't in the forefront of your mind. As sad as that is to say and recognize, it is imperative for us as believers and sufferers of hardships of the world that we need to develop a relationship with God where our first line of support and defense is to run to Him. Not to run to drinking, or that toxic significant other, or those drugs—and definitely not to the Devil.

Run home to Him, because He has a spot for you; He always does.

I am also referring to the invisible location, meaning the location that is completely and totally inside of our heads. Sounds unconvincing, right? How can we have a specific location in our head? Allow me to explain. When we are anxious, we tend to go to the things that are worldly: the lies, the tabloids, the things the world tries to make you believe, the things that make you doubt, when we really should be turning our focus and compass toward the Lord and His truth and Word.

It's all based on location. I can personally say that at this point in my walk with Christ and in my journey with my anxiety disorder, that I know for a fact that my anxiety is worse and is present when I am not close with the Lord. During breaks from school, for example, I work a lot just like most college students do. During this time of working, sometimes I am working roughly thirty to thirty-five hours a week to the point where I find it hard to make that time for the Lord and then I become more and more anxious.

That is something I have found in my personal walk and I hope that you will learn about your walk with Christ as well. Even anxiety or stress that is just present from time to time could flare up when you lack quiet time with the Lord for a period of time. It is a very risky thing to do, to be without the Lord, but once you come back into His forever welcoming arms, you know that you're home.

It is also important to keep in mind that we are never forgotten. The Lord knows us by name, and He knows where we are every single second of every day.

Picture this: God is holding His iPhone in Heaven using Find My Friends and He has you on there. He knows where you are. It's a forever and eternal scenario that never ceases at any point, and I think that is an incredible truth and promise that we get to hold on to.

The Lord sometimes will speak to us in unconventional ways, just to get the message across. With that being said, don't forget that the Lord can truly speak to you and give you your answer to your prayers in those unconventional ways. It may be something like a sunrise or sunset, a thought about Him knowing your location via Find My Friends, or a post on Instagram that moves you beyond belief. If you feel the Holy Spirit and are at peace, it's God. He's speaking to you. Regardless, just trust and know that He loves you no matter what and that you are safe.

Even when we seemingly walk far away, thanks to the pain or nervousness we feel, we can always trust that He will welcome us home with open arms, and He still knows where you are in this moment. You may think that He had forgotten, but He had not. He is with you and has been with you every single step of the way in your life.

You may not be that close or far in your walk with the Lord, so you may be finding this information thought-provoking. I pray that you will realize the truth that I hold onto so near and dear, especially during the harrowing periods of anxiety. Just knowing that, during your periods of loneliness, there is a Father out there who loves you beyond belief and protects you at all costs is a truly powerful and comforting thing.

What does location look like in terms of our friends and family here on earth?

This is an interesting and thought-provoking question that doesn't have a lot of context. That's what I'm asking; I want you to think.

I want you to visualize the times that you immediately check your phone to see the location of someone so you can know if it's a good time to call them when you need them. I want you to think of how it felt to have their support. I want you to think about how it felt for you to hear someone tell you that they are always here for you.

But what does this actually MEAN? Being HERE for you? I have a few explanations. It means that they are here for you for you to text them, FaceTime or Skype them, call them, etc. It means that they are willing and ready to serve you by being a listener and advice giver. It means that while they may not always be sitting in the chair across from you, they are always a text, call, or prayer away.

For Andrew Sweat, this is an important concept and idea for him. He shared with me how when people he knows are dealing with things, such as depression, he always lets them know that he is there for them. He feels as though that is his God-given purpose, to serve and be kind to others when they are dealing with hardships in life.

Even when he is busy, he is always there for people, and I find that truly remarkable. It is so common in this day and age to let the busy seasons sweep us away and pull us from the place we're supposed to be. It could be by helping others, just like Andrew did, or it could be by receiving help in order to build the kingdom and to better ourselves.

Sometimes, you may feel alone. You may feel shame because of your sins, because of your pain. You may feel alone and like you truly have no one. This is all false, and it is a false doctrine the Devil drives into our hearts. You are never alone.

The Lord will never forget your location. The Lord provides safety all of the time for us, because He knows exactly where we are every single day and He is right there beside us! Also, isn't it amazing to think about how the Lord has already paved the way for each and every day?

He has seen your steps, He knows what's going to happen, He knows when it will happen. To know that we have a Father who goes before us and clears the path and gives us that peace provides me with so much peace. It is such an essential fact to remember whenever you're stressed, anxious, depressed, or going through anything. Just to know that He is there and that He is with you is a surreal fact, but you should believe it because it's true!

Psalm 4:8 NIV: In peace I will lie down
and sleep,
for you alone, Lord,
make me dwell in safety.[32]

---

32 Bible Gateway. (2019). Bible Gateway Passage: Psalm 4:8 – New International Version [online]

And at night, we are called and able to lie down and to sleep in His perfect safety. You are always safe when you are with Jesus. Your heart is safe, your mind is safe, and you are safe. Anxiety and depression have no room to creep in because God has you so heavily wrapped in His arms, providing the utmost safety.

Even when you feel as though you are being drug into temptation or moving into a big new change, look back. Look at your location, look where you once were. Did you like that old time? It's time to move to freedom. Free your hearts; free your minds. Your heart does not deserve to be bound by the chains of anxiety. Anxiety does not deserve a primary spot or location in your mind. Anxiety deserves to be in the trash at the end of the driveway. Anxiety deserves to be cast out and removed.

Let the Lord free your heart and bring you away from those chains of despair. Remember that where you are right now is not a defining factor of where you will be even ten minutes from now. Even in the next ten minutes, you could have a growth so large that it changes who you are instantly. Your faith could double. Just don't quit moving and don't succumb to fear when the locations change quickly.

Isn't it pretty neat to think about how the Lord has a permanent GPS on us? He knows where we are. I know I have said that many times, but it is just such a powerful fact to remember and think about. It is so powerful to be able to come to the Lord and to know we are home when we fall back into His arms. Every single day brings new joy, so chase after it. The Lord already knows when and where you will find that joy, and He knows it will always bring you back to Him.

You are never too far gone. He always knows where you are, and He truly has counted your steps and knows you by name. Trust that He will deliver you from that anxiety and move you through the ashes and rubble of the hard times before.

END OF CHAPTER TAKEAWAYS:

BIBLE VERSES:
- Psalms 4:8 NIV

QUOTES:
- "Anxiety shows that we are too close to the world, and too far from God." – John Piper

QUESTIONS FOR REFLECTION:
- Looking at the above Bible verse and quote, what is your immediate takeaway about anxiety, and your perspective about such things?
- How does Psalms 4:8 ESV connect to the idea of safety? What does this spark in your own heart with regard to anxiety and mental health?
- How will you challenge yourself to stay restful and stay connected to God all the time?

ACTIONABLE TAKEAWAYS:
- Put a reminder in your phone to rest by having a daily quiet time. Set up a time you can commit to, whether

that be in the morning or at night. This time can differ day to day.

- Take some time away from your phone, laptop, screens in general, or anything that is or can be a distractor. Do this as a way to focus your heart on God's plan for YOUR life, not to focus on anyone else.

PRAYER:

Hey God. Tonight I lay these burdens down to You, and I feel You in the stillness and closeness in this moment. I feel You here, and I know Your goodness. I pray that You will stand next to me in this fire, and stay with me through it all. I pray that You will keep me on my toes and hold me accountable to spending time with You. You are good. Amen.

CHAPTER 11

SURROUNDED

James 4:8 NIV: Come near to God and he will come near to you. Wash your hands, you sinners, and purify your hearts, you double-minded.[33]

When you hear the word "surrounded," what do you think of? Do you think of giant droves of people being around you? Do you think of something unpleasant or pleasant? Whatever you're thinking, put a little twist on it.

Imagine that you were surrounded by a bunch of believers at a worship concert. You're surrounded by them, all of these devout Christians throwing their hands up in the air and expressing their gratitude for what the Lord has done. In the midst of all of these believers, you can't help but be

---

33 Bible Gateway. (2019). *Bible Gateway Passage: James 4:8 – New International Version* [online]

surrounded by your heavy thoughts. The difference is that you're surrounded by them internally. Your past is weighing on you, and you can't help but wonder why God would still love you even after all that has happened to you. You feel surrounded by all of these amazing and wonderful people who know Jesus so well, and you just feel like you are unworthy of being in that concert hall in that moment. You feel the void in your heart stir, but you don't know what that feeling is. You don't know what God is showing you or what He wants you to do.

Then, picture this scenario. A guy comes up to you and tells you that you both went to middle school together. He remembers you, and he said that you have been in his heart for so long now, and that seeing you at that concert just proves to him that God is God. He asks you to hang out and go catch up after the concert, so you do. You pour your heart out about all that has happened, and he sits there in awe because he firmly believes God stirred his heart to reach out to you and pour into you. This transcends into a long exchange, where you meet all of his friends and a bunch of loving individuals. You end up being surrounded by a good, positive, loving, and nurturing community.

Now, that kind of surrounding doesn't sound so bad, does it? It sounds like the thing you have always wanted, either consciously or subconsciously. It is now in your presence, and you know that this is God. This is God pouring into you and bringing you a group who can pull you up from your past, your hurt, or anything else. Just to be that consistent group in your life that we all desire deep down. Your community could be through a church, club, ministry, therapy group, family, friends from high school, or even a sorority. Personally, I'm in a sorority at Clemson called Sigma Alpha Omega and it is the best community I've ever been a part of! Your community can be anything and it can be from anywhere. If you've never had this kind of group, then trust that you don't have to search all of the ends of the earth for it. It could be right in front of you; just pray about it if you can't yet see it.

2 Corinthians 5:7 NIV: For we live by faith, not by sight.[34]

When I talked to one of my sisters, Maci Bolin, from Sigma Alpha Omega (SAO) and Fellowship of Christian Athletes (FCA), I heard a story about how dealing with a tough, toxic, and abusive relationship shaped her faith and molded her to be who she is today while also allowing her to find a positive community. In her relationship, she dealt with being abused and coerced into doing things she had no desire to do, and she was not in the best community at this time. She was friends with a lot of people who did illegal things, such as consistent underage drinking on the weekends. She met a guy who ended up being her boyfriend, but it was a very awkward and hurtful situation. During this time—and Maci has given me permission to state this—she was sexually and physically assaulted over a span of three months. During this time, she described her situation as causing her to "be angry at God, and I hated God for a while." Thankfully, this

---

34 Bible Gateway. (2019). *Bible Gateway Passage: 2 Corinthians 5:7 –
New International Version* [online]

situation ended when her unofficial yet exclusive boyfriend started seeing another girl and they broke things off.

Maci then broke the chains and went to CAPS—the mental health service on the Clemson University campus—for therapy. Maci says, "I had a history of mental health [issues]. I just never had seen anyone for this. I had always had panic attacks, I always had insomnia, I had depressed thoughts and self-harmed throughout high school and into college. When I went to therapy and started talking about stuff, they said, 'Yeah, you probably should have come a lot sooner.'"

When I heard Maci talk about this, I was in awe. There is a reason that God works through us in these situations and brings us to the reception desk at our doctor's office at certain points in our lives. He knows when we would especially benefit from these teachings and assistance.

Maci's therapists asked her a golden question that I want to relay to you: "Who do you have in your life that you can to go who you trust with stuff?" At this point in Maci's journey, she didn't really have a close group of friends or anyone she could trust with her burdens. Her "friends" would never pave a way for her to really open up and explore these kinds of topics, and she felt like they wouldn't care to just listen about her struggles. Maci was at a point in her life where she was scared: "I was afraid to tell my parents or anyone because I didn't want them to see me differently. So CAPS helped me to get out of the mindset that people won't care. And I just slowly started opening up to people and got to know people better in my small group for FCA and for SAO and it just helped so much. It blows my mind to this day how much has changed just in the past two years."

That's the thing about God: He can do the absolute unexpected in a small matter of time. He will bring you through your worst trials, and you will be clean, happy, and healthy on the other side.

Like we see in Maci's story, we are sometimes fear-stricken to open up to others, seek help, or just trust others with our own personal struggles. In fact, in 2014, only 53.9 percent of Americans sought treatment for their mental health disorder, possibly out of some type of fear or shame, according to research conducted by Bradley University.[35] We feel as though we are unworthy and that we don't deserve to receive help. There is always an underlying fear that comes from the Devil that says we will never be happy again and that we will never find our group of people.

If you feel alone right now and like you don't have a group, take it from Maci's story and know that cutting the negative people out of your life will allow for positive and wholesome people to join it and fill those voids. Maci persevered through this time in her life and continues to use her testimony as a means to encourage others to find that community. It just takes one small step—whether it's joining a Christian sorority or fraternity in college, going to a campus ministry at your high school or college, meeting friends for coffee for a

---

35   "Mental Health in America." 2019. Bradley University Online. September 24, 2019.

Bible study, or reaching out to new friends on social media and just explaining yourself.

Don't look for that positive Christian community and community of supporters in a dark place. Don't search for them at a frat party; don't search for them at a bar. Search for them in the nights when thousands of people crowd inside buildings and worship Jesus for an hour and half, like FCA at Clemson—which is the largest in the nation. Search for that group of girls in the oldest building on campus and join that sisterhood—or fraternity if you are a guy, of course. Search for that community where the heart is valued, the mind is sacred, the body is loved, and the Word is present.

Finally, due to Maci's involvement and the Lord working within her, she was able to open up to her team that went on the Costa Rica missions trip for FCA in December 2018. She was able to tell them the full story—from the depressive thoughts to the abuse and more—and was able to trust them and allow her God-given testimony to be brought down from the rafters and brought to the hearts and minds of her team, her brothers and sisters in Christ. An important message from Maci is how she felt after she told her testimony: "On that trip, the Lord showed me that opening up can make things so much easier on yourself, because you're not keeping it all bottled up to yourself, and you're not keeping it just between you and God, but you're sharing it with other people, so that they can help you but also so that you can help them."

That is the ultimate thing right there, y'all. Being able to help others and they can help you. By sharing your story with the community around you who cares and loves you so much, you could really change someone's life. Someone may deeply understand the pain, struggle, and misery you have dealt with and they may be able to help you in the end. This is what comes from sharing your testimony and allowing others in.

God has used Maci tremendously throughout her time at Clemson, both in SAO and FCA amongst all other interactions she has made, and I am proud of her story. Remember that everyone will be proud and support you for your openness, and while some people may not fully understand your story, they will appreciate and value you so much. It just takes one brave step to allow for millions of other brave steps to fall into place.

The Lord will allow you to be brave and to share your story and to get help when needed. He will surround you with the positive community you need; you just need to trust in Him and trust in His promises and fullness. Trust that He will make a way through your dark path and that He will shine a light on the community and group who will pour into you and fill your heart.

END OF CHAPTER TAKEAWAYS:

BIBLE VERSES:
- James 4:8 NIV
- 2 Corinthians 5:7 NIV

QUESTIONS FOR REFLECTION:

- When reading Maci's testimony about how a terrible situation led to her finding God and finding a good community, how does that impact you?
- How can you relate to feeling God's mighty presence right around you, even when you are going through a major trial?

ACTIONABLE TAKEAWAYS:

- Pray about finding this community if you don't have one or pray about strengthening your current one.
- Reach out to people you go to school with or work with about grabbing some food together or going to see a new movie. The more people the merrier, but definitely start with a small group or just one friend if that makes you more comfortable.
- Remind yourself when you are feeling lonely that you are not lonely and that there are always people around that love and support you.

PRAYER:

Hey God, I am really thankful that you have given me the opportunity to pursue this community and the strengthening of it. I am excited to see how you work through my life as well as the lives of others. Thank you for all you do.

CHAPTER 12

FOLLOWING THE ROAD LESS TRAVELED

———

Life is a journey. Sometimes that's all you can say about things; you're just going through a journey of sorts and it's kind of hectic. You feel like you are on a bumpy roller coaster that is going 110 miles an hour at points, and it is simply terrifying. Sometimes, this journey can be positive, meaning you are really feeling the support from family and friends and you feel satisfied with life.

You know those moments in life when you feel like things are just too hectic and will truly never slow down? You feel like you are being blindsided by all of the events and craziness that are flying right by you? All of the tests, grades, appointments, emails etc. all stack up and become a lot. It's very easy to let these things cause your brain to go into a scramble—meaning stress is heightened, anxiety is through the roof, and your mind is generally racing like a 110 mile per hour fast ball.

However, we are not called to live a life that's full of the worries, the mind-boggling instances, and the fear. We are called to live a life of peace, and we are called to turn to our Creator when things get too hectic.

Macey Coulter describes herself as having anxiety issues that weigh on her at random times: "I always finds comfort in reading Bible verses and going to church because I know that it's like home and I like reading Bible verses that give me a sense of calm whenever I'm anxious."

Jeremiah 29:11 NIV: "For I know the plans I have for you," declares the Lord, "plans to prosper you and not to harm you, plans to give you hope and a future."[36]

This Bible verse proclaims promise, and it declares to us, from the Lord, that He has plans for us that are so much greater than we could ever truly imagine. It gives Macey a great sense of comfort and a sense of direction to know that there is a plan even when she is feeling lost during those trials, struggles, and anxiety-filled moments. The Lord calls us to rely on Him and to turn to Him when we are shaken by fear or filled to the brim with doubt.

---

36 Bible Gateway. (2019). *Bible Gateway Passage: Jeremiah 29:11 – New International Version* [online]

We are called to reach out for His white robe every single step of the journey that we are on. More often than not, we may not totally know our journey, and we may not know what the outcome will look like. You could be on the brink of finding out about a job or internship you applied for, or another major opportunity. All of these journeys are so complex and beautiful, but that's because of all of the steps that are made toward your final destination, the answer is prayer. Don't forget that during this time the Lord will provide with you with essential skills and answers to prayers that will play the role into the creation of your higher purpose. While we don't always know every step of the way, we are able to find comfort in knowing He is always right there next to us during our times of struggle.

One day I was scrolling through my Facebook feed, just taking in all of the dog videos and hope-filled posts I saw. Then, I came across a post from a Christian Mental Health Facebook group I am in, and it shook me to my core and led me to think about our various journeys throughout life. Life is such a complex thing, but the thing that truly gives me the most comfort of all is knowing that God is right there with us, always. He is the One who knows every single step we will take, and He knows about every single journey that will come our way.

Over the course of our lives we are thrown into mysterious places, with new faces, and new stories to learn and tell. These journeys can be quite frustrating or just flat-out pleasant and enjoyable. We don't always know what exactly will happen, but I think Grace Werner gives an epic God-given viewpoint on this with her poem "Olive Leaf."

"Olive Leaf" – *Gracie Werner*

Opening the door to the past,
    feelings pains that are regrets, pushing the key inside,
    turning slowly to the left side,
    shaking hands reveal that darkened dusty place.

You step inside to the place that is unfamiliar to your
    mind's fragment place.
    Thoughts, fears twirl in a tremendous world.
    Then, it hits you like a big rushing wave – shocking,
        relentless terror.
    It's becoming overwhelming to bear.

You cover your eyes from that darkened, unfamiliar place.
    Peeking ever so slightly between the cracks of your
        fingers, you want to go back.
    When you turn around, the light
    has been consumed.

You're walking ever so cautiously down that dark path, not
    even trusting yourself.
    You turn around calling for someone's help.
    Its deadly silence closes in on its prey.

Then light streams through it all, words of hope.
Like the dove that brought the olive leaf.
    My lips, crying out with all of my life,
    "Lord, my Father and friend, is that you?"
    I fell to my knees with all the strength I could bear.
    I folded my hands saying a silent prayer.

Lying with my face to the ground, I praised the Lord to the
    extent of passion that I just had to let go.
I love you with all that I have in my heart.
Crying with everything that flooded from fear, I gave it
    to the Lord to carry for me,
Asking forgiveness of doubt and fear. He touched my
    cheek with caressing love,
a care that lived deep in His eyes.
"My lamb I had lost you but now you are found." "Come
    with me because you are my lamb and I have found you
    even in the darkness of your doubt."

John 8:12 NIV: When Jesus spoke again to
the people, he said, "I am the light of the
world. Whoever follows me will never walk
in darkness, but will have the light of life."[37]

Whoa. Grace Werner really told it truthfully here, and it is
amazing. First and foremost, it is incredible to see how God
would speak that through someone in order to share this
truth with us in such a vivid and visual way. When I first saw
that beautiful work of poetry, I was taken aback because it is
so real. It is so vivid, and you can visualize this happening
right as you read it. I have personally had this experience
before, where you feel so lost from God because of your mental struggles, and then one day you just collapse right back
into His arms. It is such an incredible thing.

---

37   Bible Gateway. (2019). Bible Gateway Passage: John 8:12 – New
     International Version [online]

We see and can even feel how Jesus would "touch my cheek with caressing love, a care that lived deep in His eyes." We understand this because we know that all along our journeys and throughout our lives, we are looked and viewed in such a loving manner by God. He loves us so much, and He cares about us. On your journey you may feel as though you have lost sight of God, but never fear because He is still there with you. He never leaves, and He is always right there. Like proclaimed in the poem, "I have found you even in the darkness of your doubt."

Y'all, He is the soul searcher. He is the searcher. You may be new to this whole "Jesus thing," or you may be an old friend of His; you may be trying to find it for the first time or trying to find it again. Wherever you are in your life, He will find a way to find you. He will find you in the midst of your crying as you wait for that phone call, He will find you as you hide in the darkness of your fear and pain that has succumbed you for so long. He will find you where you are on your journey, and He will love you just the way you are, because He made you and created you to be the human you are.

This is such a great kind of love, and we all deserve to feel it. We deserve to feel this kind of love and presence on every single step of our journey, even if it's just a tiny baby step. Once you fully accept Jesus into your life and run back into His forever open arms, you will feel this love. Your journeys will become a little more bearable—not necessarily easier, but definitely bearable because you have the peace you need to move forward.

No matter what path you go down on this journey, He will always be there. He will always make a way.

Psalm 119:105 NIV: Your word is a lamp for my feet, a light on my path.[38]

Let Him light your way down this path. Let Him light your way through that doubt and fear about getting help for your pain and mental suffering. Let Him light your journey to your true destiny. Allow Him to show you His Word and speak to you through everything you go through. Read the Word, and let His Word move through you. He will lead you, by lamp, through the darkest shadows, the hardest nights, the unimaginable moments. He will lead you, by lamp, through the happiest moments, the victories, the "I made its." He will lead you.

Wherever you are right now, whether you're reading this in your bed at home or in your car at night, please know that the Lord is calling you to step out of your comfort zone and abide by faith. He will be right there with you every single step of your journey, and He is ready to catch you if you stumble and fall. He is ready to shine a light on your feet to show you the dangerous serpent that is at your feet—fear, doubt, hatred, or just a real, live snake. He is ready. Let Him in. Let Him lead you through this journey.

---

38 Bible Gateway. (2019). Bible Gateway Passage: Psalm 119:105 – New International Version [online]

END OF THE CHAPTER TAKEAWAYS:

BIBLE VERSES:
- Jeremiah 29:11. NIV
- John 8:12 NIV
- Psalm 119:105 NIV

QUESTIONS FOR REFLECTION:
- Think about a time you took the uncommon route. Think about how this impacted you and allowed you to grow as a person and in your walk with Christ. How does that impact you today?
- How do you want to tackle the next, or current, journey in your life in a more Christ-centered way?

ACTIONABLE TAKEAWAYS:
- In your gratitude journal, if you have one, or even on a clean piece of paper, write about a journey you have been on. To be creative, make drawings depicting it. Look back on it when you were in a time of confusion to see how things were during that one point, and how you have truly made it through.
- Pray about having faith despite the odd twists and turns that occur along this path.

PRAYER:
Heavenly Father, I am incredibly thankful for all you have done for me on this journey. I feel as though I am dodging waves left and right to get to this point, but I am thankful for you and that you have pulled me through it all. I am praying that during this season of life that you won't let

me forget your goodness and good works that you have provided. Remind me to stay focused on You even in the midst of this trial and all of the twist and turns. Amen.

CHAPTER 13

LAND OF THE FREE—
BECAUSE OF THE BRAVE

———

The few, the proud, the strong. The ones who serve our country. The ones who protect our flag and our great nation on
a daily basis. The ones who served in combat and protected
us. The ones who have the great privilege of saying, "I am a
member of the United States Armed Forces." The ones who
see the worst, but also anticipate a hopeful outcome. The
ones who put on their boots, strap on their vests, and run
straight into the horrors we run away from and see only on
television. The ones who have that American flag on their
arm, and God in their heart.

These brave few who put their lives on the line for us aren't
immune from mental health issues. According to data from
the US Department of Veteran Affairs, 41 percent of Veteran's
Health Administration (VHA) patients have been diagnosed

with a mental health disorder.[39] They struggle, and we witness it when we see veterans begging for money on the side of the road. We see it when we see veterans not receiving the treatment that they deserve. We see these brave men and women every day. It's time to realize that while there is a stigma against mental health in general, it is time to end it. It's time to end it because it impacts millions of Americans daily, including our veterans.

John 15:13 NIV: Greater love has no one than this: to lay down one's life for one's friends.[40]

One afternoon while working on this book, I had a surge of American patriotism run through my veins. I feel as though it was the Lord speaking through me, and I thought of a man in uniform with whom we are all very familiar. His name is Chris Kyle; may he rest peacefully. I decided to do a quick Google search and find anything and everything I could about his walk with Christ.

One thing we don't really see a lot in the movie *American Sniper* or hear about a lot in general is Chris Kyle's belief in God. According to the *Washington Post*, he definitely had a belief and a strong faith. Kyle writes in his book:

---

39 Office of Suicide Prevention and Mental Health, United States Department of Veteran Affairs, (2017). *Suicide Among Veterans and Other Americans 2001–2014.*

40 Bible Gateway. (2019). Bible Gateway Passage: John 15:13 – New International Version [online]

"I'm not the kind of person who makes a big show out of religion. I believe, but I don't necessarily get down on my knees or sing real loud in church. But I find some comfort in faith, and I found it in those days after my friends had been shot up. Ever since I had gone through BUD/S (SEAL training), I'd carried a Bible with me. I hadn't read it all that much, but it had always been with me. Now I opened it and read some of the passages. I skipped around, read a bit, skipped around some more. With all hell breaking loose around me, it felt better to know I was part of something bigger." [41]

I firmly believe that Chris Kyle carried a very important message that we should all be inspired by: despite all hell breaking loose around him, he knew that he had a God that was greater than those fearful times who was watching over him and his comrades. The Word proved to be something that gave Kyle a lot of peace and calmed his mind down from the hardships that would come at him. It is noted that he kept a list of important priorities which was mentioned throughout *American Sniper*: God, country, family. He kept these priorities straight and kept God at the center of it all. According to an article that was released in 2013 by Nicholas Schmidle of the *New Yorker*, Kyle kept his faith during the Iraq War and has a red crusader's cross tattooed on his arm to show the world that his faith was at the center of his life.[42]

41   Sarah Pulliam Bailey | Religion News Service. 2015. "Here's the Faith in the 'American Sniper' You Won't See in the Film." The Washington Post. WP Company. January 14, 2015.
42   Schmidle, Nicholas. 2019. "In the Crosshairs." The New Yorker. The New Yorker. July 10, 2019.

While we see Kyle's prominence in the War on Terror, it is little known (yet unsurprising) that he was a strong advocate for the mental health of veterans and co-founded an organization that brings awareness to mental health disorders, specifically PTSD. PTSD is post-traumatic stress disorder, and it develops following a traumatic event. In this case it is due to what was seen and heard on the battlefield, but for others it could stem from traumatic childhoods, relationships, natural disasters, etc. Chris Kyle aimed to help these veterans by enabling them to ease their tensions and the pain with which they were dealing. Sadly, his death brought a lot of focus to PTSD in a way that was unintentional. A veteran suffering from PTSD was the one who killed Kyle and his buddy, Chad Littlefield, at a gun range. It was common for Kyle to take his friends who were suffering from PTSD out to a shooting range to let off some steam, and this time it ended fatally for Kyle.

While it is definitely harrowing for us to know that we lost such an amazing American, we still see how his legacy is living on today. His stories of how his faith impacted his life, how he kept his Bible in his pocket at all times, and his passion for helping people who suffer from mental disorders live on. Chris Kyle will never be forgotten, and all he has done for our great nation will forever live on.

This shows the impact of mental health disorders in another way as well. The veteran who killed Kyle and Chad was also a sufferer of some mental health disorder, according to *ABC News*.[43] This shows the impact of untreated mental health

---

43 Katie Moisee | ABC News. 2013. "Former Navy SEAL Chris Kyle's Killing Puts Spotlight on PTSD."

disorders; no matter what form of disorder individuals have, we can see it. We could see this lack of treatment due to drug addictions, alcoholic behaviorism, even sometimes lost jobs and lost opportunities. Untreated mental disorders present themselves in hard but present ways that have lasting impacts over people today.

Isaiah 40:29 NIV: He gives strength to the weary
and increases the power of the weak.[44]

Next up, I wanted to add a snippet of something my friend, Andrew Boyles, mentioned to me about his grandfather who served in the Vietnam War:

"My grandfather died in the Vietnam War, saving some of his men from a fire in an ammunition dump. You have no idea how much I would have liked to know him. And yet, in his death, I feel that he taught me more than he ever could have in his life, as he showed me what true selflessness and courage is, and he showed me how to put others before oneself. He showed me what a good leader does, and by imitating him, I hope to be a good leader in this life of mine. I love my grandfather, and while I never knew him, he still impacts my life in a positive way to this day. It cannot be called a good thing that he died, and yet he taught me much even in his terrible and untimely death."

---

44 Bible Gateway. (2019). Bible Gateway Passage: Isaiah 40:29 – New International Version [online]

Thinking about mental health in this sense, I garner a vision of strength and courage from Andrew's grandfather. Serving in the military, no matter the situation (war or just day-to-day activities) is a large mental game. It requires grit, toughness, and a strong, hard head that gets you through it all. We see that here in all of our military and our veterans, and it impacts people to this day. Andrew describes that while he wishes that he could have met his grandfather, he knows that he served this country and his people in a positive way. This also shows the mentality of positivity, and how it is important to focus on the good in situations, even in the worst of all times.

In times like these, it is important to thank not only our veterans but their families as well. Their families also pay a price; they see their loved ones go through some of the hardest and most life-altering things. It's through these times we are called to love, encourage, and show grace for the ones who struggle. It is imperative, because these men and women struggle and deal with more things than meets the eye.

Isaiah 6:8 NIV: Then I heard the voice of the Lord saying, "Whom shall I send? And who will go for us?" And I said, "Here am I. Send me!"[45]

---

45   Bible Gateway. (2019). Bible Gateway Passage: Isaiah 6:8 – New International Version [online]

There is a man in my life who has a prominent influence over me, my family, and anyone who comes in contact with him. He is a joyous man, a Marine veteran who served in Okinawa, and who has timeless stories to tell. This man is my great-great-Uncle Harold King. He is ninety-five years old and is still as sharp as a needle.

I had the privilege of chatting with him on the phone not too long ago, and it brought back such a comforting and happy feeling. When we talked, he told me that one of the biggest and most important things to remember is, "Power is found in the Holy Spirit." This is a very impactful message, and you will understand why in just a moment.

Uncle Harold mentioned how it is important for us as believers to live out the Word in our daily lives by praying and allowing God to move in our lives. Uncle Harold described it as such: "You can go to church seven days a week but until you accept Jesus's plan and the Holy Spirit ... that's where the power and contentment comes from."

Uncle Harold grew up going to church, and he was only nineteen years old when he was drafted in the Marines. He served in Okinawa, and while discussing his time serving in World War II can still be tough, we can learn a lot from him by his walk with Christ.

For several years, Uncle Harold would give the invocation before the NASCAR race at Darlington Speedway. According to a 2008 *New York Times* article about Darlington Speedway, Uncle Harold "has been the most constant presence during race weeks over the past fifty-eight years." When I asked him about the speedway and his invocations, he said that he would always "speak from his heart" and that "the freedom of being able to share the Word is important. The message is there for people to see the message in you. Talk to them, don't preach at them."[46] It is so important for us as Christians to speak what the Holy Spirit has put in our minds and hearts. Whether it is just being kind to one another or speaking up about something that has been nagging your heart and mind, speak from your heart.

Furthermore, I feel that this relates to mental health as a whole, but specifically therapy. This therapy could be either group or individual therapy, but these therapists aim to talk to people, not preach at them. They ask patients questions to provoke thoughts, and the intent is to never hurt people. I know this personally from my experience of receiving therapy at CAPS, and it is true: I never feel peached at. As Uncle Harold says, it is essential to talk with others but to not do so in a way that is preaching at people, because this could scare people off. In my opinion, this could be why there is such a stigma against therapy … because people see therapy unrealistically portrayed in movies or shows as people being preached at; or, due to past experience, someone may feel fearful to attend therapy.

Remember, most therapists, especially if they are highly recommended for treatment of your specific disorder or illness, will talk to you in a way that makes you comfortable and that doesn't involve preaching at you in a dictatorial way.

---

46 Branch, John. 2008. "The Track That Defied the Writing on the Wall." The New York Times. The New York Times. May 10, 2008.

When we think about speaking from our hearts, one thing that came to mind to me while writing this chapter and thinking about Uncle Harold and his wisdom is that it is so important for us to be kind to one another. If you feel that kindness down in your heart, share it. Utilize that as a prime tool to love on people around us, you never know who may need it. It is so important for us as believers to shine our light in the lives of others and to be kind, and to speak from our heart.

From time to time, it is very common to have something come in our mind and heart and to feel it so deeply. It almost feels like it's nagging, in a sense. It begins to drive you crazy sometimes, but that could mean that the Lord wants you to notice it. He desires for you to speak out this truth and this wisdom He has instilled in you. That is exactly what Uncle Harold is saying: that we need to speak what's on our hearts. Whether that's in an invocation, whether that's to a minister or therapist, whether that's to a family member or friend, we are called to speak what's on our hearts.

Speak what's on your heart when you go to the therapist or when you turn to God or a family member about something that is weighing you down. Don't let the lies of the past or fear of judgement turn you away. Speak what's on your heart, and people will hear you. They will understand the highs and lows you are going through, and they will commend you for what you say to others.

The Holy Spirit instills this power and might in our hearts, and creates that stillness and voice within our minds to go and speak the Word and His heartfelt and tender message the Lord provides.

Always remember this, as said by Uncle Harold himself: "Keep the Lord in your heart and everything will go alright. Let the Lord lead you, cover you, and everything will be all right." This is such a true statement, and it humbles me to hear that from a very special veteran in my life, and to know that everything will truly be okay as long as we keep the fear of the Lord in our hearts.

Everything will always be okay, even when it doesn't seem like it. Keep the Lord close, and let Him work through you.

END OF CHAPTER TAKEAWAYS:

BIBLE VERSES:
- John 15:13 NIV
- Isaiah 40:29 NIV
- Isaiah 6:8 NIV

QUESTIONS FOR REFLECTION:
- If you come across someone who is in need of support and help mentally or physically, how will you aid them?
- How have you seen God work through your life with regard to being able to speak to others about what He has done through your life?

ACTIONABLE TAKEAWAYS:

- Practice talking to others in a way that isn't preaching at them and build positive relationships with the people around you.

- Write the saying by my great-great-Uncle Harold, "Keep the Lord in your heart and everything will go all right," on a sticky note as a daily reminder for you during the hard times in your life.

- Thank a veteran for what they have done for our great country, and thank a current member of our military for what they do.

PRAYER:

Father, today I am standing in front of you with my mind wide open, ready to receive your wisdom. I strive to listen and to be able to lend a helping hand to those around me, but I can't do that without your grace. I pray that you will give me the ability to carry conversations with grace and to be able to continue on forward despite the hard things that come my way.

CHAPTER 14

KING OF MY HEART

—

Philippians 4:19 NIV: And my God will meet all your needs according to the riches of his glory in Christ Jesus.[47]

The song "King of My Heart," written and performed by Bethel Music, is one that is simply so powerful. It is a song declaring against the evil that our God will never let us down, and that He will never let us fall. He is always there, and He is truly the king of my heart.

I just want to give you some personal background on something that has been a part of my life for the past year or so now. I have dealt with several issues within romantic relationships. It's something of which I'm not particularly ashamed or proud. I'm just going with the Lord's divine plan.

---

47 Bible Gateway. (2019). Bible Gateway Passage: Philippians 4:19 – New International Version [online]

During this plan and time frame, I have learned a lot about myself and about my faith. I have learned a lot about my anxiety and how to handle that, including potential triggers that could be things within relationships. I have found that if a guy does not provide reassurance when you ask for it, he isn't worth it. I have also found that if a guy says some really harsh and hurtful things constantly and has no remorse, you really need to remove him from your life immediately. Pretty obvious stuff, right? Yeah. I feel like I went over mountains and boulders to find this out, and not to mention having to find the courage to break off toxic relationships. I did it, and I survived. I felt free the moment immediately after I ended it.

Friends, that is something first and foremost I want you to hear right now. I want you to know it is okay to cut off toxic people, to end toxic relationships, and to put yourself first. Pray about it, and keep your faith and eyes on Him during this process, but He will never let you down.

Luke 6:28 NIV: …bless those who curse you, pray for those who mistreat you …[48]

You need to remove those toxic people from your life in order to let the Lord fully into your heart and reign as the King of your heart. Some of the lyrics in the song talk about protection, and how we desire to have the Lord be the shadow where we hide, and the mountain we run and turn to. I think

---

48 Bible Gateway. (2019). Bible Gateway Passage: Luke 6:28 – New International Version [online]

that's a wonderful visual because it gives us that peace, feeling, and knowledge that we're truly secure and safe under His wings and perfectness. When I really think about those lyrics, it reminds me about how truly BIG and POWERFUL He is. Our God is mighty, and He is our shadow. He is the one we can run to and trust that His arms will be wide and outstretched, ready for us to rush into. He is not only our King, but He is also our Father.

The Lord knew every single move and every single word that would be spoken throughout that relationship with the guy who ended up hurting me. The Lord knew, but He protected me. I prayed; He spoke. I acted; He delivered. The Lord is almighty and mighty, and He was the place I ran to, under His wings.

I may feel that someone or something has a special place in my heart, and while that is true, no one here on earth is the king of my heart or gets to have complete control of my heart. The Lord is the One, the only one, who has that kind of level and amount of significance in my life. The Lord breathes life into my lungs, and helps my heart beat day in and day out. He is the One who wakes me up. He is the one who teaches me, through His Word, experiences, and testimonies about how to love others truly. Among all of this, the Lord is the true King of my heart. As all of the blood rushes through my veins, His grace continues to pour deeper and deeper, rushing through my veins.

If you give someone too much room in your heart and push the true King out, it will cause you anxiety and stress. It will make you worry and fear. It will cause major sadness if that person is removed from your life—meaning if you gave them such a stronghold on your heart, you will feel like you have no one left. While it is important to love others, it is also important to protect your heart and to remember that it belongs to the most high. It doesn't belong to the little boy down the street, or the girl you met at the bar; it belongs to Jesus. Remember that Jesus is the One who will remain forever. Do good and protect your heart.

I have been saved. I am saved. I know I will be saved again in the future. It is an incredible moment when you experience being saved, and I will detail my story in a moment, but the Lord saves us numerous times. Ever since the moment I truly came to the Lord and laid down my life for Him, in a mature fashion, I have still been saved and rescued many times ever since. It is truly a powerful thing. I am not at all belittling your personal story, but never forget that the Lord will continue to save and rescue you from the things that trespass into your heart and mind.

I grew up in a Christian home, and we went to church on Sundays fairly often. When I was in my freshman year of high school, I went to FCA, Fellowship of Christian Athletes, at my high school for the first time. I did this after I saw a post on Instagram about it, and I thought it seemed interesting. It definitely piqued my interest, so I thought, "Well, I'm starting out in high school, I definitely need to get involved in something and this seems like the way to go." So, I went to FCA the next morning at 8 a.m.

I remember feeling hungry in that moment. Not just hungry for food, hungry for MORE. More of the Lord, more of His grace, everything. I wanted it and I needed it bad. Two days later, on Sunday, I decided to go to the youth group at the church I grew up in. I went and that was the first time I ever heard the song "Oceans"—I grew up going to a more traditional service within the church, so those types of songs were not sung—and it changed me forever. There is nothing wrong with traditional music, but the language of the songs was difficult for me to understand and internalize. I never could get into this music as much as I can with the modern-day Christian groups and singers that evangelize and worship today. There is always something super powerful to me when I hear the sound of guitars, acoustic or electric, and voices singing the praises for Jesus in a more modern-day feel.

I specifically remember hearing it and just hearing those words and knowing that that was where I was meant to be in that moment. Moments later, the youth band sang "Set A Fire." That was the moment. The moment that rocked my world and changed my life forever. It was truly in this moment that, when I was begging for Jesus to set a fire in my soul, that I felt at peace. I felt the Holy Spirit consume me, and I felt so present ... so alive.

It was that simple moment that changed my life. Stepping foot into FCA that one Friday morning changed my life and led to me attending my youth group that Sunday. The Lord uses one moment to rock your world, to change your life, and to lead you. It was in that moment when the Lord truly became the King of my Heart. It was in that moment when my hunger led to something else. It led to a heavy desire to pursue a relationship with Christ. Friends, it just takes one moment. One prayer. One sigh and some shouting. Just a little bit of something, and the Lord can use it to change your life. He is a really amazing God. He is the one who shows up and works in unconventional ways.

Let the Lord in. Allow Him into your heart. Find that hunger for Him and for His grace. The Lord wants it, but He also wants you to know it does not take much for you to come home to Him and pursue that relationship. He is always right there with you. Protecting you from harm, guiding you through the forest. Allow Him in and know that He will never let you down. He will mend your brokenness. He will see your anxiety; He will see your pain. He will fix it and lead you through the wilderness.

You will go through tough things in life. That is common, and normal. You will still go through tough things even after, and despite of, your close relationship with the Lord. Those situations are the Lord testing you to see how faithful you will be in those times and to see if you will run away or cling to Him.

Let me take you way back in this book ... envision you're standing on a ship in the middle of the ocean. It is storming and you feel like you don't know where to go, where to hide. The Lord is still with you. Even when the ocean stills, and the wind passes on, He is still with you. No matter your location, no matter your stance, no matter how hurt or broken you are, He loves and wants you.

Sometimes, I feel unworthy of His grace and love. I knew that the Lord worked through me to allow me to have the strength that enabled me to break up with a toxic boyfriend, but some of the words that that guy said to me sometimes would make me question how worthy I am of the Lord and His grace. I don't really know why that is, but it would, and that was the moment when I knew I had to end it with him.

If there is one thing I pray and hope you will get out of this chapter, it is this: if someone is making you feel unworthy in any way, shape or fashion, you need to cut them off immediately, especially if it's making you doubt your worth in Christ. You do not need to stay with someone or stay friends with someone if they make you feel dumb, broken, or unworthy. Friend, I promise you that you are worthy. You are worthy of the Lord's grace. You are valued and loved by so many. Do not let one person tell you otherwise.

The Lord will always stand as the King of my heart, and I hope He will stand as the King of your heart as well. I hope you will continue to seek after a relationship with Him like I did, and that you will prayerfully pursue that relationship with Him. He is good, and He will never let you down.

Making the decision to fully accept Jesus as the King of my heart was the best decision I have ever made. My anxiety disorder had a stronghold on my heart that would cause my heart to stir because God knew that He wasn't the ultimate King of my heart. He knew that. He wanted in, though. He needed those toxic relationships gone in order to heal me from my anxiety. By having Jesus as the King of my heart and believing that and trusting that fact daily, I have truly seen how my anxiety has lost its hold. Anxiety itself is scared to come into my heart because it just knows that it will be trampled and removed because Christ fills my heart. His love has filled every broken part of my heart and mind.

Let Him in. Let Him remove the shackles of depression. Let Him fill your lungs with air and let Him fill your heart with warmth. He will make a way; you just need to allow Him to take your heart and mend it. He is the true giver, the Savior. He will become your song, your joy, your prize. He will become the One who can mend that broken heart after someone toxic is removed, but then He will mend it and shape your heart and mind to realize how this is beneficial in the long run.

Trust in Him and know that what good He has done for me and for others, He will do good for you as well.

END OF CHAPTER TAKEAWAYS:

BIBLE VERSES:
- Philippians 4:19 NIV
- Luke 6:28 NIV

QUESTIONS FOR REFLECTION
- Is God truly the king of your heart? How do you know?
- How do you personally plan to keep God at the center of your heart and mind?

ACTIONABLE TAKEAWAYS:
- Remove toxic people from your life. If you have been thinking about it but are hesitant, this may be the time to remove them from your life. Removing those toxic people

from your life doesn't need to be done in a harsh way; it can be 100 percent silent, or even just involve removing the hold people have on you.

- Remember that God is forever and that He is always present with you.
- Write yourself reminders on your phone or laptop, or even just on a good old sticky note, to have daily quiet time with Him, where it is just you and Him.

PRAYER:

Hey God. Today I am praying to you that you will allow me the vision and focus to keep you at the sole center of my heart and that you will protect me from swaying one way or another, in terms of negativity. I am praying for strength and also for courage during this season of life, and that I will be able to hold true to my heart that you are the King of my heart. Amen.

CHAPTER 15

BEAUTIFUL CREATURES

———

You, child, you are beautiful. Put down that mirror, put down that eyeliner; you are beautiful and worthy with or without the makeup. Step off that scale; you are beautiful and worthy no matter what it reads. Come out of the bathroom; you deserve to feel full. You are worthy. You are beautiful. You are talented. You were created in the image of God.

No matter the scars, no matter the past, no matter what, you are amazing and valued. You deserve a place in this world, we need you here.

Genesis 1:27 NIV: So God created mankind
in his own image,
in the image of God he created them;
male and female he created them.[49]

---

49   Bible Gateway. (2019). Bible Gateway Passage: Genesis 1:27 – New
International Version [online]

Out of the dirt and ashes we were formed, and we were made human. Adam, the first man. Eve, pulled from his rib, the first woman. We are made in the likeness of God. We see how God sent His one and only Son, Jesus, to be the perfect image of God. Jesus shows us how to live out the image of God, and how we are supposed to live as Christians: living as servants and showing the goodness of God throughout our daily lives.

Being a Christian, we are called to not only love others, but to also love ourselves. One thing that has been prominent in my walk with Christ and journey through my anxiety disorder is how I would always do things to be a people-pleaser and would hardly take time for myself or even stand up for myself. I ended an extremely toxic relationship and once I did that, I knew that was me loving myself. That relationship was one that at times would make me feel less beautiful or worthy due to the words that were said to me, and once I ended that relationship, I felt content and felt beautiful. I felt like I had done something for myself, and that was because I truly loved myself enough in that situation to yank myself out of it, by God's grace.

It's not just by protecting ourselves that we can prove to ourselves that we love ourselves, but also just by our treatment of our bodies and minds. This is also something I have learned by going to therapy and by just going through and growing from the situations that life would throw at me, curveball style. While the cutesy pictures on Pinterest of "self care" are important (you know, the foot lotions, aromatic candles, cuddling up and watching a movie, etc.) and should not be mocked, self care should be practiced in other ways too. One way to practice self care is to think at the end of the day of what happened, acknowledge what you're grateful for, and look to what you will do tomorrow if time allows it. Also think about what God has done in your life, and about how you are worthy no matter the nature of the day's events.

So often we get swept away into what presents itself on social media, the perfect looking lives with the perfect relationships, trips, etc. and we feel as though we aren't the same or even as beautiful or worthy as them. Why is that? I don't have a great answer for that besides the solid answer that what we see on social media is solely the highlights of others' lives. We are seeing the good moments of someone's life, and while it is imperative for our own well-being that we don't constantly post sad things about our lives on Facebook (it's more important to take these matters up with God, a trusted family member or friend, or a therapist), it is good to get real from time to time. Our lives are not perfect.

There are days when you will just be glad you got up and took the garbage out to the can, and that is great. You are still worthy. There are days when you will get home from a day of work that took you pleasantly by surprise and that is great. You are still worthy. There are days when you will get off the bus and walk into your apartment with tears streaming down your face because of something you saw in the news, and while that's sad and awful, it doesn't mean you're any less worthy or any less beautiful because you have mascara streaming down your face and because you had a hard day. You are still worthy.

What we see online is sometimes not true reality. We all have some chub when we sit down. We all get "food babies" from time to time. Ladies and gentlemen, this is life. We may not feel perfect all the time, but remember that this is what's real. You are made in the perfect image of God, and that is what matters the most.

One go-to for my friend Celeste Marchant, from Sigma Alpha Omega, is to listen to worship music. "I feel the most beautiful when I worship God." This is when you are at your rawest, purest form. When you step down and bow, literally or figuratively, before your Savior. When you thank Him for what He has done, and what He will do in days, months, and years to come. He knows who you are, He knows you by name. He created every single inch of you, and He designed you and molded you into His perfect image. You are so tremendously loved by Him, and that is something that is worth praising.

To Celeste, feeling beautiful means "feeling loved, from myself, God and others." What Celeste shared here is super powerful and needs more mileage. It is important to her that she feels love from herself AND from God. So often we miss one of those two components. Think about this, God WANTS and DESIRES us to love ourselves and to realize that we were made in His image. While this can be a very difficult thing to wrestle with and accept, it is imperative.

Comparison is a thief. It is a thief of joy, thief of happiness, and thief of peace. Do not let it pull you from God.

Celeste also shared her incredibly humbling testimony with me, and I am honored to share it with y'all. It is incredible to see how she has defeated an eating disorder that haunted her heart and mind for two years, and to see how God has freed her from those shackles and chains. Celeste suffered from exercise bulimia and anorexia nervosa. This means that she would work out a ton and she felt the need to look an exact certain way, and she didn't eat fried foods or sweets over the course of two years. This instance really overtook her mentally and caused hardships within her relationships with others and God.

One of the most powerful parts of her testimony is this:

"Sometimes I wonder how I escaped that part of my mind … and the only thing I can think of is a memory that will forever stick out to me. I was baking cookies with my sister during Christmas time—a process I enjoyed yet I never allowed myself even one chocolate chip from the cookie dough—and all of a sudden, I realized how happy I was. In that moment, as I took the cookies out of the oven while I danced around the kitchen in my fuzzy socks, I was so overcome by joy it was as if my mind no longer had room for any obsession, pain, or hopelessness. For the first time in almost two years I had dessert. I was not filled with regret or shame, because my heart was already consumed by this radiant joy that I cannot explain other than to say God must have had his hands in the cookie dough. God must have had enough of it and took matters into his own hands, because to this day I have not gone back to that dark, silent, colorless place."

Now there you go, y'all! Look at how God has worked in Celeste's life, and look at how He put His mighty foot down and said that enough is enough and gave her that freedom.

During this time, she was suffering tremendously from something the Devil sent into her heart, and God defeated the Devil in His triumphant way and delivered Celeste from her chains and gave her freedom.

Celeste and I pray that when you look in the mirror you will remember that you are so loved and beautiful. I know sometimes it truly is hard to accept that, but even if you need to do sticky note reminders daily on your mirror just to remind yourself of your worth, I highly recommend it. If you are in a season where you are struggling with self-worth, write on a sticky note something you love about yourself each day. If you find that you are really vibing with your smile two days in a row, write it! Stick these notes on your mirror or wall and look at them each day when you get ready or whenever you just need a hype up. Actually read them though; do not make it just a quick glance. It helps to have a Bible verse or two as well, the ones that really mean a lot to you, on there as well.

Keep sticky notes wherever you are, on the scale, on the mirror, wherever, just keep them there. During these seasons you may be in, or maybe when you're just struggling with self worth a bit, push yourself to see the good in reality. It is so easy to be negative about ourselves and it can be difficult to be kind to ourselves, but challenge yourself to see the good in you. Hop on that scale and when you see that number, be PROUD of yourself and LOVING of yourself, because you, my friend, are beautiful and are so worth loving. No number can ever change that. You are awesome and amazing just the way you are.

Pray about it. The key to success and just overall contentment in life is to pray. Give these worries and struggles to your

Father, and pray about it. He is there and He wants to help you from your hard place, and He will give you the peace of mind that you need to move forward and to trust in Him consistently. The Devil himself will try his hardest to still your joy and to make you feel bad about yourself, but don't let him in. Instead, blast that worship music and sing praise to the One True King.

Celeste shared one final thought that resonated with me deeply, so I will share it: "I have found that the greatest refuge from insecurity and self-hatred is the open arms of God where love is never ending and acceptance knows no bounds. Once you start loving yourself, you can love others, all because of the eternal love of God." In all things, trust Him. In all things, seek Him. In all things, love yourself no matter what faults happen, or what imperfections you believe you have. Trust Him, and be grateful for His everlasting love.

His goodness and graciousness can pull you out of a dark tunnel, just like it did for Celeste. Never lose hope, and never forget that you are so beautiful. You, child, are fearfully and wonderfully made.

Psalm 139:14 NIV: I praise you because I am fearfully and wonderfully made; your works are wonderful, I know that full well.[50]

---

50 Bible Gateway. (2019). Bible Gateway Passage: Psalm 139:14 – New International Version [online]

END OF CHAPTER TAKEAWAYS:

BIBLE VERSES:
- Genesis 1:27 NIV
- Psalm 139:14 NIV

QUESTIONS FOR REFLECTION:
- What makes you feel beautiful?
- What do you do to remind yourself of your beauty?
- When you feel less than worthy, how will you remind yourself that you are amazing?

ACTIONABLE TAKEAWAYS:
- On a sticky note, write a word that best describes you. Keep it just in one place, or in many places—whether it be your bathroom, mirror, closet door, or even in your kitchen, give yourself that reminder.
- On the lowest days, instead of picking apart your appearance, find at least one good thing that you like each day. For me personally, my smile is the thing that I choose even when I feel like I don't look good. Find something each day to flip that flow.
- Remind yourself of the Lord and how He created you in His perfect image, and how He loves you no matter what. He knows you are beautiful.

PRAYER:
Hey Father. I am praying to you to thank you for your good works, and to thank you for giving me this wonderful life. I know that sometimes I question my worth and I feel as

though I am not beautiful. I pray that you will give me the confidence and restore the hope I have. Thank you for making me in Your perfect image. You are so good. Amen.

CHAPTER 16

LAY YOUR BURDENS DOWN

———

One of the hardest things to do in life is to let loose and to give complete control of a problem or painful experience in life to someone else. It is hard to accept that our burdens are not meant for us to wrestle with, but rather for God to take control over and work with. Our burdens are truly not our own. Jesus can cast our fear and give us perfect love and grace overall.

One of my dear friends, Amelia Sizemore, from FCA and Clemson Dancers, shared her testimony with me and I thought it was important to share. While hearing her testimony, it really clicked with me about how important it truly is to cast and lay our burdens down at the feet of Jesus. We wrestle with these things so much and it gets harder and harder each time, so it is imperative that we give it all up.

Philippians 4: 6-7 NIV: Do not be anxious about anything, but in every situation, by prayer and petition, with thanksgiving, present your requests to God. And the peace of God, which transcends all understanding, will guard your hearts and your minds in Christ Jesus.[51]

"In eighth grade, I was doing way too much. I was competitively dancing twenty hours a week, in All-State Band, All-State Chorus, and on top of that, I was bullied by two girls. By the summer, I was diagnosed with a general anxiety disorder. For three and a half years, I was on different medications. This made me complacent in my faith and angry. I was going through the motions with my faith. During my senior year of high school, I got off all medication and felt like myself again. I felt like a fog was lifted off of me. Coming to college, I was anxious and scared, but excited for a new chapter in my life. When I got to college, I felt rejected for who I was. I was dropped by twelve sororities the very first round of recruitment and was rejected from a dance team I tried out for. However, I joined Kappa Alpha Theta and loved it and found a great group of friends during my first semester.

"I learned that my worth does not come from the letters I wear, it comes from the Lord."

51 Bible Gateway. (2019). Bible Gateway Passage: Philippians 4:6-7 – New International Version [online]

Ladies, for those of you who are in a sorority, this is an extremely important pointer from Amelia that we need to focus on. I know everyone has the certain sorority they have to get into and if they don't, they will be crushed. This is understandable because it is a goal and it's normal to be upset by missing a goal, but don't forget that the letters you wear do not match the worth that comes from God. Your worth is truly not found in the letters but in the God-given sisterhood that will teach you and allow you to learn about yourself and more about Him. Remember, there is no match for how worthy you truly are.

Amelia further said:

"I finished my first semester strong and loved Clemson. However, when I came back for spring semester, I noticed my freshman friend group was not living a life uplifting to the Lord. They were going down a path that was not going to be a healthy place where I could grow. When I decided to leave this friend group, it caused me a lot of anxiety. Then I went to Memphis through an FCA mission trip and it changed my life. It was the first start of Christian community for me and it was the first time I felt freedom from anxiety. As freshman year came to a close, I was unsure of my place in my sorority. I did not know if it was worth it to stay in Theta.

"That summer, I worked at Winshape Camps as a camp counselor. The clearest I heard the Lord's voice was when I was tucking in my campers with a flashlight, the Lord told me that I was going to be the light in Theta, so I decided to stay. The start of sophomore year, I was hall manager for Theta and honestly was lonely. During this time, I was unsure of my major and was having a lot of testing anxiety and panic attacks during tests. My cousin passed away and my family was having a lot of medical issues too. And, on top of all of that, my sorority was shut down. As hall manager, I had convinced all these girls to live on a hall that we did not have. During this time, I learned what it meant to lay my burdens down at the feet of Jesus. He taught me how to rely on him and to find joy in all situations. He showed me his love for me, no matter how many people rejected me. No personal rejection can ever exempt me from God's love for me. During this hard time, I saw the most growth in my faith and saw the most of God."

Amelia really tackles an important issue here, and one phrase I love is, "No personal rejection can ever exempt me from God's love for me." This is so important, y'all! In life we will be rejected by partners, companies, sororities or fraternities, etc., but that does not mean that you are rejected by God. These rejection letters are just proof that that door is not the one God has intended to open, and that it is not a part of your plan. He is pushing you to work or be somewhere else that will allow you to learn more about Him, and that is worth being uncomfortable.

Laying your burdens down at the feet of Jesus means so much to Amelia, and it means so much to me as well. It means laying all of the unknowns, the fear, the anxieties, and everything known to man down at His feet. If it is causing us worry or fear, lay it down. Stress? Lay it down. It goes for everything. If it is not God-glorifying and you are trying to figure out how to work and get out of this problem, lay it down. Everything that happens in your life, lay it down. The Lord will bring you through the waters and out of the deep trenches and He will push you to be a light for the people around you.

When Amelia laid her burdens down, she began to realize how to truly find joy in all situations that she was in, no matter how ugly or bad they were. When I laid my burden of anxiety down at His feet, I began to realize and learn how to effectively cope with and manage it. They say it can't be done and that mental health disorders can't be healed, but with my God I know they can be. You just have to trust in Him and trust that what He says will be done.

If you're feeling like you're drowning in a season of busyness, pray about it. The Lord will truly pull you from the darkness and the shadows and He will bring you to the light. He will bring all the bad that happens to the light, and He will heal you from it. The depression you are experiencing will soon pass, so long as you trust in the Lord. Everything you deal with will be made right. If it isn't here on earth when it happens, it most certainly will happen one day when we reach the pearly white gates of Heaven.

Matthew 11:28 NIV: "Come to me, all you who are weary and burdened, and I will give you rest."[52]

---

52   Bible Gateway. (2019). Bible Gateway Passage: Matthew 11:28 – New International Version [online]

Now, when you're actually thinking about "laying your burdens down," you may not really know how to do this. Do this by praying that He will release you from whatever chains and bondage you are currently trapped and held by, and by praying that you will be delivered from all of your woes and fears. Pray that He will teach you how to be an example for someone going through the same season you are.

Remember, no anxiety, depression, PTSD, bipolar disorder, etc. are any match for our God. God triumphs over all, and with a lot of trusting Him, and a lot of laying your burdens down, He will release you and He will protect you from the thieves that threaten to come by and snatch your joy.

Rest, child. Take up your cross, bow down, cry if you need to, stand up, dust yourself off, rest. Rest and know that He is Lord, the One who is ready to heal you, the One who is ready to give you rest upon request. He will release you from those shackles, just like he did for our Savior, Jesus Christ. Be brave and lay your burdens down. The journey is just starting, the healing is just beginning, and the freedom is everlasting.

END OF CHAPTER TAKEAWAYS:

BIBLE VERSES:
- Philippians 4:6-7 NIV
- Matthew 11:28 NIV

QUESTIONS FOR REFLECTION:
- Do you normally carry your burdens, or someone else's? What does that feel like for you?

- How can you let go of your burdens and give them to God?
- Do you believe that God can truly take away your burdens?
- How have you seen God heal you from your struggles, and how can you help someone else through that healing process?

ACTIONABLE TAKEAWAYS:
- Reflect on the hard times that ended up being positive when God took away your burdens.
- Pray, and pray consistently.
- Whenever something unfortunate comes up, give it to God. Pray it away and let Him handle it. Allow yourself to remember that you may have to tend to things that are happening with regard to said burden, but the burden is not yours anymore.

PRAYER:
Heavenly Father. I am stuck. I am in a place right now that I am not proud of. I am here, and I need You. I have way too much weight on my shoulders … it feels like thousands of bricks are piled one by one on my shoulders and back. I have too much on my mind. I feel my mind becoming jammed with negativity. Father, I need You. I need this release, and I need to feel You here. Please help me from this hardship. Amen.

CHAPTER 17

WHAT DOES FAITH MEAN TO YOU?

"WHAT DOES FAITH MEAN TO YOU?"
I want you to wrestle with this one for a minute. What exactly does faith mean to you? Is it the ability to believe in someone and trust that they will be there? Is it a religious thing? Is it having faith that your favorite football team will win?

What does faith come down to for you? Is it just a word you throw around or does it hold a significance greater than one can possibly imagine?

Faith to me means that I can trust God and know that through all things, including the anxiety and stress-filled trials in my life and the happiest moments, He is good and He will deliver me. He will teach me His ways and teach me how to live like His Son, Jesus.

By having this faith, we are saved. We are saved because we rely on Jesus and trust that He will guide us through the storm. He will move us past the quicksand and the tides that threaten to envelop our hearts and minds.

Ephesians 2:8 NIV: For it is by grace you have been saved, through faith—and this is not from yourselves, it is the gift of God.[53]

It's not just something we do. It's something we pray about, work for, and ask for. We ask for our God to give us that faith and ability to pour into our hearts and minds and to do the incredible and unimaginable. It's not about us; it's about glorifying Him.

Much of the time while I was writing this book, I talked about faith. My faith grew tremendously during the publishing process, due to having to raise $4,000 for my campaign to help fund the process. It was incredibly challenging, both physically as I would stay up late by sending messages as outreach (and not to mention the times my eyes hurt so much from staring at my screen), and emotionally as the process became draining when I initially did not see my desired results. It took a ton of time, but I eventually kept climbing that mountain, like Coach Dabo Swinney said, and made it to the top all by God's grace.

It was during those rigorous thirty days that turned into sixty days—because of a God-given time extension on the

---

53 Bible Gateway. (2019). Bible Gateway Passage: Ephesians 2:8 – New International Version [online]

campaign—that my faith grew so much. I was able to reach out to friends and family I hadn't spoken to in a long time, I was able to learn so much about others, and I was able to see how God was working in my life. There was a moment when I was crying hot tears about having seven days left on my campaign and I was nowhere near making the $4,000 and Brian Bies, my awesome publisher, gave me an extension. I also cried tears of PURE JOY when I was able to witness the unthinkable happen: at least ten people pre-ordered my book within an hour and a half after I posted a very heartfelt message about the book campaign extension.

When I would text Brian feeling worked up in fear because of the campaign, he would counteract those fears with words of encouragement, including sending me the phrase, "You will publish," at least fifteen times in a text. It was so meaningful to me and it gave me a lot of encouragement. My point is, faith is put in God, but it can be put in a person as well. Brian had faith in me that I would publish my book, I had faith in myself that I would get my revisions done, and I had faith in God that He would allow me to spread the word to all who needed to hear it.

I had faith that my campaign would hit $4,000, and it did in the most incredible way. I had faith through it all, and God delivered … and now you have this book in your hands.

For this book, I decided to challenge others by asking them what faith means to them. I received a lot of responses and they morphed into something big and beautiful. It's incredible to see and witness how people's faith has grown just through the struggles that they go through every day. You know what they say, "Grow through what you go through." I feel like that applies here heavily.

SAVING GRACE

Faith is so much more than just some cheesy slogan on Pinterest, as Hannah Fortune says:

"To me faith is so much more than just all of the cliché quotes you see on Pinterest, Facebook, or Instagram. Faith is all about knowing God is with you always, in all ways. From your biggest triumphs, to your worst hardships, and all of the mundane moments in between, He is right there alongside you. As a sophomore in college, I've definitely had more than my fair share of the good, the bad, and the downright ugly, and just even knowing that God was a constant that I could always rely on got me through so many things. Some of the biggest tests my faith has had to endure happened within the first couple of weeks of my sophomore year of college. From spending so much time and energy focusing on a friend who was, and still is, going through major mental health issues, to dealing with the aftermath of my mom being in a car accident that could have killed her, I felt exhausted and depleted. My faith in God and His plans for me and my loved ones was my lifeline. I'm so fortunate that my faith was rewarded; my friend is on the road to recovery, and my mom survived her accident without even so much as a scratch. So yeah, to me, faith is more than a Pinterest quote; it's an absolute necessity and a saving grace."

Her faith during the hardships in her life, such as the terrible wreck her mom was in and her ability to help a friend with her personal battles, has allowed Hannah to grow tremendously. What stuck out to me the most is how she describes faith as a saving grace. Thinking of faith in that manner is very true, and very raw. It shows how faith truly is all you have at points. For me when I deal with my anxiety, I think of faith as being my saving grace as well. It is truly all you have at some points in life.

GOD'S PLAN

God's plans for our lives is something that gives great comfort to many, including my sister, Elizabeth Radecki. When I asked what faith means to her, she said, "Faith is trusting in God's will for your life. It's also knowing that He already has it all planned out for you!"

Faith means a similar thing to Elizabeth and so many others, including my sophomore year college roommate Amanda Breakfield. She said, "What faith means to me is that no matter what happens I know that everything happens for a reason and that God has a plan for me." Both Elizabeth and Amanda make the important points about how God knows everything that is going on in your life, and it is all part of His plan. The anxiety, the fear, the worry, and the stress—all of it is 100 percent in His plan.

TRUST

Faith is about trust as well. It means that there is either an underlying trust in someone—maybe you have faith that your friend will follow through with bringing you chips and queso like they promised—or an underlying trust in God.

You have faith that He will do the unimaginable in your life and that He will work no matter the hardships. For my friend Jonathon Rhymer, this resonates with him: "Faith means that I can have complete trust in someone. Faith is something to guide me and to fall back on when times get hard."

Various seasons of life throw large unknowns at us, and it is important that you keep your faith during these seasons. Whether you are starting a new chapter or you are just going through day-to-day life, it is imperative to keep the faith. Like Jonathon says, it's all about trusting someone. Trust that God will deliver you and pull you from the hardships you currently find yourself in. By having faith and carrying that weight, He will move you forward and will allow that trust and faith to grow.

My friend Jack Lenhardt has a similar view. To him, faith is "believing in something you don't see, like trust. In a trust fall, you can't see the person behind you but you believe that they'll catch you when you fall. Similarly, God catches us when we fall and teaches us lessons that [help] us grow for the future." While you can't see trust itself, you can see it being played out. We see it in this analogy and visual of God catching us in a trust fall, but we also see it when we are confident and able to trust a friend with an important bit of information.

Similarly, a special individual in my life, Ethan Whitman, also says, "To me faith means that when I feel as if all hope is lost I have something or someone I can look toward and know they will help me. From praying, to talking to certain loved ones about what is happening. To just going with the flow and keeping my chin up and thinking positive." To him faith also is imperative in having the ability to talk to someone about the things going on in our lives. He, like many others, can trust that someone or something will be there to help during the times of trouble.

Faith is also having the ability to trust that God will pick you up when you are down in the dumps for a while. I can totally understand this. After dealing with hardships with anxiety, even when I am in the midst of it all, sometimes I will feel my mind clearing like the clouds when they part from a heavy rain shower. I feel a beam of light come in from the Sun and warm my heart. In this case, the light is God. When my mind clears, even when I am lying in bed feeling exhausted because of the wear and tear anxiety causes, I am able to tell the Lord that I know He will pull me out of this misery again.

**

Isaiah 58:11 NIV: The Lord will guide you always; he will satisfy your needs in a sun-scorched land and will strengthen your frame. You will be like a well-watered garden, like a spring whose waters never fail.[54]

---

54 Bible Gateway. (2019). Bible Gateway Passage: Isaiah 58:11 – New International Version [online]

In your season of growth, you will witness God pouring into you in so many ways. He fills our cup, He fills our hearts, and He fills our minds with all of the positive and healthy things that are so worth sharing.

Be a watered garden, and don't be afraid to show and share your faith with others. By keeping the faith, your bones will be made strong. What was once lost will soon be found again, and all of the scorched pieces of your heart will be calmed.

BELIEVE WITHOUT SEEING

For my lifelong best friend, Grace Ehlers, "Faith to me is believing without necessarily seeing. No matter how hard life gets my faith remains constant... . Sometimes even strengthens as well. I don't have to see God face to face to know He's always right by my side. Isaiah 58:11 'where God guides, He provides.' Life can be scary, but at least, I can have faith knowing God has it all under control." Even when you feel that you are lonely or ashamed, keeping the faith means believing in the unseen. We see how God works daily, but the unseen is the closeness and incredible proximity of God during these hard seasons.

This also resonates with my former coworker Kathryn Murphy, because to her, having faith means "fully believing in the unseen. It's trusting in the one that is not physically there but you can feel him when you need someone. Faith is when nothing goes right but you know it will end up in a perfect plan because God is in control of everything and says in his Word he will never leave us. Faith is putting your life and your trust in the one and only God you can't see because he has control of everything and can see the future that we wish we could."

Grace provided a great summary of Isaiah 58:11, in that where God guides, He provides. It is important to trust that even when He leads us through the darkest tunnels, He will still provide along the way. He will provide light despite the harrowing darkness we feel in our minds or hearts. He will provide the food we need when we are lacking. He will provide a home for us. He guides, and He protects. Just like we read in Isaiah 58:11.

2 Corinthians 5:7 NIV: For we live by faith, not by sight.[55]

PRESENCE, COMMITMENT AND BELIEVING

My friend Katie Griffin also agrees that faith is about believing in the unseen and trusting in someone, but she also takes it a different perspective, one of presence and commitment. When asked about what faith means to her, she said that it is "trusting in God even though I can't physically see Him, I know He is there. Faith is hearing a voice and knowing it is God. To me, faith isn't only believing in God, it's trusting that He is always there. I think faith is also a commitment that we make. When things aren't going the way we think they should, that's when

---

55 Bible Gateway. (2019). *Bible Gateway Passage: 2 Corinthians 5:7 – New International Version* [online]

we show our commitment to God by staying faithful and trusting in Him and His timing." Like Katie mentions, as Christians we are called to be committed to Him. We are called to stand firm in our faith even when the waves are roaring beside us.

Being committed is a huge part of faith, and it is all about trusting in Him and knowing that He is the promised One who will deliver us from all things. Keeping this commitment can be a bit of work. This work includes praying, trusting, staying in the Word, building a community with other believers, and keeping our faith strong.

My friend Patrick Regan agrees that while faith is something we work for, it is also something we are aware that we are following. We believers all have a reason behind our following, and that is because we know God and His goodness. We know that He sent His son to die for us on the cross. It is up to us to put our best foot forward and to work toward faith, and to know that God will be there through it all.

One important and very simple concept of faith comes from my friend Carlos Evans. To Carlos, faith means "having a strong belief in God, and to trust Him with your all your mind and spirit." This idea of faith is very important. Faith is 100 percent trusting in God and having that strong belief in Him. It's knowing that He can do the unimaginable even when it seems unlikely that it will happen.

CLARITY

Finally, having faith gives my friend Katy Trawick a sense of clarity. As mentioned with the visualization of clouds parting after a storm, that is the kind of clarity that Katy envisions. To her, it means that while we may not have all of the answers or know what to do all of the time, we know that faith is there, and we have faith that God will see us through. While we may not know how we'll do on that presentation in our history class, or on the manuscript we have worked on for years, it's about having faith and seeking that special sense of clarity that will deliver us forever. Katy says it best: "Sometimes I don't always have the answers or know what to do, and faith gives me clarity." This is so important for us to realize and ponder. While we don't always have all of the answers to every single problem that comes our way, we can trust in Him that He will provide us with the clarity we desire.

It is truly inspiring to me to see how faith has worked within the lives of others. To see how God has provided that faith for many people's lives is amazing, and is definitely displayed here. To keep faith during the dark times, the happy times, and everything in between, no matter how spontaneous or out of the ordinary this faith is, it is such an amazing thing. The Lord always provides for us, and He provides that little lesson on faith. He teaches us about how important it is to trust in Him and to keep the faith.

Matthew 17:20 NIV: He replied, "Because you have so little faith. Truly I tell you, if you have faith as small as a mustard seed, you can say to this mountain, 'Move from here to there,' and it will move. Nothing will be impossible for you."[56]

As stated in Matthew 21:21 NIV: And Jesus answered them, "Truly, I say to you, if you have faith and do not doubt, you will not only do what has been done to the fig tree, but even if you say to this mountain, 'Be taken up and thrown into the sea,' it will happen."[57] This is truly an amazing thing that Jesus communicated to people's hearts and minds, and it relays directly back to what we are thinking about here. Think about how powerful that is to know that your faith, even if right now it is as small as a mustard seed as in Matthew 17:20 NIV, can really change your life to that large degree. No matter how large or small your faith currently is in your life, by just keeping the faith and believing and trusting in God you can change your whole life.

Take that step and know that your faith in God is right there with you. Have faith that God will see you through your hardships, because we know He will. We know that He will push us through the dark holes of depression, the racing thoughts of anxiety, and the flashbacks of PTSD. All of these

56 Bible Gateway. (2019). Bible Gateway Passage: Matthew 17:20 – New International Version [online]

57 Bible Gateway. (2019). Bible Gateway Passage: Matthew 21:21 – New International Version [online]

are no match for God, especially when we have such a strong faith in God. Mountains can move, and they will move. Just trust in Him and have faith that He will do what He has promised.

It is all about keeping a positive mindset during your hard times. What all of these individuals told me about their faith greatly inspired me. It shows me, and I hope it shows you, that faith can be used in any way, shape, or form. It can be used in the greatest ways.

The Lord will show up and will sometimes test your faith. Throughout this chapter people mentioned times where their faith was tested but then the Lord always shows up and does amazing things—by saving, protecting, and healing.

The Lord is always with us no matter where we are. Sometimes your faith will be tested, and you may feel angry at God and ask why these things are happening, or why your anxiety is worsening. You must trust Him and know that it will all work out in due time. The Lord never leaves anyone behind. Keep pushing through and keep using your faith just like you do. The Lord will deliver just like always!

END OF CHAPTER TAKEAWAYS:

BIBLE VERSES:
- Ephesians 2:8 NIV
- Isaiah 58:11 NIV
- 2 Corinthians 5:7 NIV
- Matthew 17:20-21 NIV

QUESTIONS FOR REFLECTION:
- Does your faith have a large impact on your life?
- How do you view faith, and what does it mean to you?

ACTIONABLE TAKEAWAYS:
- Answer the question, "What does faith do to you?" and see what you come up with.
- Always remember that the very basis of faith is having that strong belief in God. Read this chapter and the passages associated with it, as well as other passages throughout the Bible, and build your belief in God. As your belief grows stronger, your faith will grow stronger.
- At the end of each week, look back on your week and assess how your faith has grown.

PRAYER:
Heavenly Father, I am sitting here in awe of Your goodness. It is so incredible to me to see how faith impacts my life but also the lives of others, and I am praying that You will continue to allow it to impact my life in a similar way. I pray that I will be able to witness Your goodness in my life even more, and that my faith will continue to grow. Amen.

CHAPTER 18

CHANGE

———

It's time to make a change. While I am no licensed therapist, I am truly passionate about the mental health field and maybe you'll see me working as a therapist one day. I have pulled from and learned from many different therapists to find tips and tricks on how to manage various mental health issues. Whether you have a diagnosed disorder or not, I truly believe that God will work through you if you just take the time to read this.

John 14:27 NIV: Peace I leave with you; my peace I give you. I do not give to you as the world gives. Do not let your hearts be troubled and do not be afraid.[58]

———

58   Bible Gateway. (2019). Bible Gateway Passage: John 14:27 – New International Version [online]

One night, I read an article in *SELF* called "11 Little Mental Health Tips That Therapists Actually Give Their Patients," just to get a little inspiration for this chapter from the knowledge of members of the professional healthcare field. I came across these important pointers:

Alicia H. Clark, PsyD said, "Most of the work of therapy happens outside the consultation room," and, "The best progress happens when you apply what you've learned outside that setting, in your real life." Dr. John Mayer PhD restates this fact, adding, "There are 168 hours in a week," and "It would be terribly arrogant on the part of a therapist to believe that your one-hour intervention will suffice to keep your clients mentally healthy for the rest of the 167 hours."[59] Ladies and gentlemen, it's time to allow God to work in our lives and to learn how to defeat these issues once and for all. It just takes a good bit of work outside of going to therapy. By making a few changes in your daily life, you can help yourself without your therapist.

Remember, the tips and tricks you are reading here are great, but nothing is better than going to an actual therapist and receiving in-person treatment and discussion. This is a great building block, but please do note that this should not replace your regular mental health care, or deter you from seeking mental health treatment and relief.

59   Miller, Korin. 2017. "11 Little Mental Health Tips That Therapists Actually Give Their Patients." *SELF*. 2017.

Through writing this book I have found that a very essential and useful way to help myself out mentally and keep myself collected is to write down my thoughts.

That sounds a little tricky, right? You may be wondering if there is a right or wrong thing to write down, and the answer is no. Whatever you put down on paper or on a digital document is exactly what is meant to come out, and you are not wrong for thinking it.

Write down a couple of positive things that are going on in your life. Maybe you saw a cute, cuddly little dog today; write that down. Maybe you got to watch your favorite TV show from years ago; write that down. Whatever it is, find the good in every day even if it is something small. Remember, the seemingly inconsequential things can be the most monumental.

One of my favorite takeaways from the *SELF* article is Dr. Clark's belief on how important it is to put a positive spin on things. We can call this "flipping the flow," as mentioned earlier in this book. It's essential to flip the flow on things that are happening in our lives, and to find the positive in every situation. Here are some examples of flipping the flow:

- Too busy and hardly have a moment to yourself? Feel thankful for a rich social life and trust that you will have a free moment soon enough.
- Waiting in a long line for something you want? Be grateful that you have the opportunity to get something you want.

For me, sometimes I'll flip the flow on having to wait in a long line for something at school by thinking about how I am fortunate to even be there, standing in a line at my dream school (go Tigers!).

Just from my own time going to therapy I have learned so many self-help tips and tricks. Some of these suggestions are below:

- Rest. Allow your body to rest. No matter what struggle you are dealing with at this point in time, allow yourself to rest.
- Challenge yourself to do one thing daily that will impact your life.
- Practice square breathing. This one is basically where you breathe in for four seconds and then breathe out for four seconds.
- Write it out. As mentioned above, it is so important to write things out. One particularly difficult day, I sat at my desk and I wrote out (and used pretty colored pens to make it more fun) everything that was on my mind. It doesn't have to make sense. It's what you need to do, so just get it out.
- Get physical. Even if that means just doing a few jumping jacks or going for a run, do whatever you need to do to get your heart pumping and blood flowing.
- Be proud of yourself for little successes. The small things can always transform and grow in magnitude, and then become a bigger win than you initially realized.
- Continue to seek and ask for help. It is always okay to ask for help. I promise you it is. No one will view you differently just because you are receiving help. These mental

health disorders are difficult, and it is really hard to deal with them on your own.

Matthew 6:34 NIV: Therefore do not worry about tomorrow, for tomorrow will worry about itself. Each day has enough trouble of its own.[60]

One of the most important things that I cannot begin to stress enough to you is to put your trust in God during this time. No matter what you're going through, pray. I know you just learned some tips and tricks on how to handle these things and to manage your mental health, but in order to make the change firmly you need to pray, and you need to accept this as something you truly want.

As mentioned above in various ways, it is still essential and imperative to seek help. Your therapist will not judge you, nor will they think any less of you. You are still worthy even when you don't see it. Everyone who knows you are receiving help will be so proud of you and they'll be excited to see your progress. Remember, therapists simply want to help. They just want to see you grow and they will do whatever they can to help you become the person they believe you can be. Therapists are the most loving people you will ever meet. They understand what you're going through. Many of those that you will come in contact with have been in this

60   Bible Gateway. (2019). Bible Gateway Passage: Matthew 6:34 – New International Version [online]

field for years and have likely seen it all. Maybe they haven't encountered exactly what you're dealing with, but they have seen and heard forms of everything.

God has gifted us and blessed us with individuals here on earth who are capable of being His hands and feet and providing us with the care, help, resources, and physical touch that will help us grow and move through these hardships. He knows that by receiving this care we will see His work and know that it is He who is working, and He who deserves all of the glory for placing these people in our lives and rescuing us from these hardships.

God will work through you as you use these tips above to work and build that firm, solid foundation for your growth, despite the hardships that weigh on you. God is going to do big things in your life, and I firmly believe that. Just hold true to this knowledge and wisdom that God has spoken through me, my therapists, and the articles I have read that allowed me to write this chapter effectively and in the exact way that God wants it to be written.

National Suicide Prevention Lifeline: 800-273-8255 (24/7)

Mental Health Crisis Hotline Number: 888-788-2823 (24/7)

Crisis Text Line: Text SUPPORT to 741-741 (24/7)

END OF CHAPTER TAKEAWAYS:

BIBLE VERSES:
- John 14:27 NIV
- Matthew 6:34 NIV

QUESTIONS FOR REFLECTION:
- What does change mean to you?
- Do you usually fear change? If so, how will you combat this fear and not let it win?

ACTIONABLE TAKEAWAYS:
- During the seasons in your life where change is prominent, keep reminders on your phone or sticky notes on your wall about motivation.
- Talk to a friend or family member about the change that is occurring in your life.
- Stay constant in prayer and maintain your quiet time with God during this time.

PRAYER:
Father, I am beyond thankful for You even though there are large amounts of change occurring in my life in this present moment. It is overwhelming, but I know You are greater than all of the moments in my life that cause me stress and pain. I am ready to envelop this change with open arms, since I know that You are here. Amen.

CHAPTER 19

SIMPLE TRUTH

Isaiah 40:29 NIV: He gives strength to the
weary
and increases the power of the weak.[61]

As you now know, my faith is a huge player in my life. It is everything; it is the reason why I get up in the morning, why I tend to have a fairly positive outlook on life, and why I am who I am. As you also know by now, I do deal with Generalized Anxiety Disorder (GAD). When I was diagnosed with GAD, I was not at all surprised, and I was very happy to find some relief and answers, but it did sting just a little bit. It stung because of how it was, and still is, a thorn in the flesh. A mighty imperfection that threatens, but does not win.

---

61 Bible Gateway. (2019). Bible Gateway Passage: Isaiah 40:29 – New International Version [online]

One day, I was scrolling through Amazon looking for some books that I thought would be really good and thought-provoking. I love to read books and am always looking for ones about faith and Christianity as a whole. I came across a book called *Stronger: How Hard Times Reveal God's Greatest Power* by Clayton King. Clayton King is a very inspirational guy; he is a teaching pastor at Newspring Church, and the founder of Clayton King Ministries and Crossroads Missions and Summer Camps. The only time I ever heard him speak was when I heard him at my high school's FCA gathering, and I was so inspired by him. I knew that when this book popped up in the list on Amazon that I absolutely had to get it, and boy am I glad I did. Once I cracked open the book for the first time, with that lovely smell of a new book (book lovers, do you feel me?), I knew immediately that I was truly meant to read this book in that moment. I knew it.

I read and read, and dug and thought. Things hit home, things cut deep, but one thing really stuck out to me. It's found on page fifty and is a passage from the New International Version of the Bible. This is what it says, typed just like I found it in the book:

"In order to keep me from becoming conceited, I was given a thorn in my flesh, a messenger of Satan, to torment me. Three times I pleaded with the Lord to take it away from me, but he said to me, 'My grace is sufficient for you, for my power is made perfect in weakness.' Therefore I will boast all the more gladly about my weaknesses, so that Christ's power may rest on me. That is why, for Christ's sake, I delight in weaknesses, in insults, in hardships, in persecutions, in difficulties.

For when I am weak, then I am strong. *(2 Corinthians 12:7-10, emphasis added.)*"[62]

Y'all, first of all. "I was given a thorn in my flesh." What's so ironic to me is that my publishers did not even know about this quote when we came up with the subtitle for my book. Anxiety is the true thorn in my flesh, but it builds me to be so much stronger. It's imperative for us as Christians to be strong no matter our weaknesses or the things that threaten to spill over and harm us. It's imperative for us to know that it is okay to not be okay, and to show others that too. That is a central focus of this book: to show that it is okay to be a Christian and to have a mental health disorder. Do not let others shame you or pull you down; you are beloved. Most importantly, having any kind of mental health issue doesn't make you any less of a Christian or mean that your faith has wavered.

This letter from Paul to his friends provides such a strong and meaningful message that I believe deserves our focus. Read this passage again.

2 Corinthians 12:9 NIV: But he said to me, "My grace is sufficient for you, for my power is made perfect in weakness." Therefore I will boast all the more gladly about my

---

62 Clayton King. Stronger: How Hard Times Reveal God's Greatest Power. Page 50.

weaknesses, so that Christ's power may rest on me.[63]

The first time I read this passage from 2 Corinthians 12:7-10 that Clayton King cited in his book, I literally felt my stomach drop. I felt my mouth hit the floor, and I felt the Holy Spirit consume me. I knew in that moment that God was speaking to me to allow this weakness to be present, but not win. To allow these feelings, to allow the weirdness and peculiarity that occurs during anxiety, depression, or just when you're going through a lot and you're feeling kind of weird.

Read that verse up there again, "My grace is sufficient for you, for my power is made perfect in weakness," (2 Corinthians 12:9). Always remember that your weakness will allow you to grow, and His grace will pour into and fill your weakness and create strength. Out of the ashes we will rise, and the Lord will be the one who propels that. It is so powerful to know that while the Lord knows what Satan has given you—the thorn—He knows and promises that His grace will be enough and will heal you and your pain. He knows that His grace can and will overcome any and every single obstacle that comes your way.

That, my friends, is the **simple truth** that I pray you will guard in your hearts and keep in your minds: that the Lord will provide grace for you. Despite dealing with something

---

63 Bible Gateway. (2019). Bible Gateway Passage: 2 Corinthians 12:9 – New International Version [online]

so hard and tragic, the Lord will still deliver you from it. He will allow you to grow through both the good and the bad, the tragic and the empowering, and the degrading and uplifting. He promises amazing things and He promises that He will always be by your side, ready to rescue you. He knows that once you let Him into your life that He can do amazing things and that His grace and presence will relieve a lot of the pressure from the thorn in your flesh. Weakness is not meant to be something that is looked down on, or a reason you should feel less than someone else.

We have all felt weak or overwhelmed at various points in our lives, and that is okay. It's normal to feel weak, but just know that the Lord will fill those gaps and fill your heart with undeniable grace and peace that will carry you forever and ever. The Lord knows that you have a thorn, and He still loves you no matter what. You are chosen to deal with that burden because He knows you will learn to hand that burden to Him, and He also knows that you will inspire and impact someone else who deals with a very similar—if not the exact same—burden that you do.

Another point Clayton King mentioned was, "We are stronger because of His strength, and His strength is on display in our weakness."[64] That is a point that I can really get behind because not only is it true, but it is also comforting. My sweet Grammy told me that she never would have known that I dealt with an anxiety disorder because I never showed it. That meant so much to me because it takes a lot

---

64 Clayton King. Stronger: How Hard Times Reveal God's Greatest Power. Page 51.

more on some days than others to stay strong and to remain positive despite the ravaging thoughts running rampant in my brain.

Personally, that is definitely when I see His strength the most: when I am dealing with a period of anxiety and I'm feeling really weak. I feel strong when I turn to the Lord and realize and feel His might during the duration of my battle with anxiety. I feel strong when I remember that the Lord will see me through, and I feel strong once I realize that the Lord is breathing not only life but also strength into my heart, mind, and lungs. It is comforting to know it will truly be okay, even when you physically may not feel that way.

Another simple truth that I have pulled from Clayton King's book is this: "The greater purpose in our weakness is to experience an intimacy in our relationship with God we could never know any other way."[65]

Boom. What a truth. Read that again.

These mental health issues, this stress, doubt, worry, fear, everything. All of it is truly allowing you to grow closer and more intimate with the Lord.

He sees you when you are shaking with fear, when you are bedridden and hopeless. He uses this weakness to ignite a fire within you to move forward and to step up to the plate, while remembering that He will heal you and that

---

65 Clayton King. *Stronger: How Hard Times Reveal God's Greatest Power.* Page 50.

His grace is mighty and abundant. When you step up to the plate, swing for the fence. Do this because you have that peace and grace within you that is from our God, and you are strong enough to do so. You are strong enough to look at your thorn in the flesh and tell it that it doesn't have a stronghold on you anymore. That thorn is no match for what our God has to say and for what our God can do. The thorn will never win.

No matter where you are, no matter how hard things are, or how good, the Lord will use you. He uses you in your weakness, and He allows these things so that you will grow closer to Him and continue to build His kingdom. I wholeheartedly believe that God allowed the weakness of anxiety to come into my life so that it would push me to turn to Him and pursue His love, so that He could pursue me right back and guide me through the dire hardships that happen in life. It is a hardship to have anxiety, and while I would not wish it on anyone else, it is imperative that we realize that sometimes these hardships are truly blessings. They allow us to have strength, they move us, and they allow for us to grow through everything with which we struggle.

The thorn will never win, God always will. The One who loves us without cost, the One who loves us no matter what we have done, will always win. Run to Him and trust in the simple truth that He loves you and He will work in your life no matter what. This will allow you to experience such an incredible form of intimacy with Him, just like Clayton King mentions. You are never too far gone to experience this level of intimacy with Him. He invites you into His arms to protect and help you through your weakness, and to provide you with strength. Allow Him to use you through this weakness and storm. It will allow you to in turn better the community around you and help others. You've got this; I know it.

END OF CHAPTER TAKEAWAYS:

BIBLE VERSES:

- Isaiah 40:29 NIV
- 2 Corinthians 12:9 NIV

QUESTIONS FOR REFLECTION:

- How does it feel to realize the truth that God is allowing our weaknesses to increase our strength?
- Do you deal with a lot of pushback with regard to your weakness? (Whether that weakness be a mental health disorder or something more general, such as not being super good at math.) How does that look for you? How are you going to deal with that pushback and counteract it with positivity and your increasing strength?

ACTIONABLE TAKEAWAYS:

- Write in your journal or on a sheet of paper everything you are thankful for, both the good and bad.
- On the same sheet of paper, write about how you think God will use you as you deal with the bad things.
- Pray.

PRAYER:

Heavenly Father, I am in awe of your goodness. I am in awe of how you love us despite our weaknesses, and you allow strength to build and come from these weaknesses. I pray that you will allow me to see the good in my weakness and allow me to build from it. Amen.

CHAPTER 20

SELF HELP

---

2 Corinthians 3:17 NIV: Now the Lord is the Spirit, and where the Spirit of the Lord is, there is freedom.[66]

This chapter is something that I wanted to write to help you if you struggle from any mental health disorder or just need a little pick-me-up, advice, or self care.

First and foremost, I want to tell you that I am so proud of you. I am so proud of how far you've come, I am so proud of your faith, and I am so proud (and thankful) for your support of this book and that you're reading it. I'm so proud of you for working so hard, and for trying your best. Days get tough, but never forget that you're bigger than your disorder or struggle. The Lord is greater than that low, and He is mightier than

---

66 Bible Gateway. (2019). Bible Gateway Passage: 2 Corinthians 3:17 – New International Version [online]

the Devil. You will find the peace you desire. The Lord will provide like always.

I'm going to share a little bit of my story. This could be slightly repetitive but here it is. In September of 2018, the first semester of my freshman year at Clemson, I developed some anxiety issues that were taking a toll on me. I really was dealing with a lot and it was overwhelming my soul. There was one night when I was sitting at my desk in my dorm, and I felt myself get anxious, extremely anxious. I do not know what provoked it, because everything at that moment was okay in my life ... no new changes or anything crazy. I prayed about this. I decided to look on the health services website that Clemson offers, and I decided to take a mental health screening test.

After answering all of the questions with honesty, my results came back and suggested that I had Generalized Anxiety Disorder. I did not take that as my official diagnosis, but I took it as a stepping stone and door opener from the Lord to go get checked out by the professionals. I went and talked with the mental health specialists on campus and I was then diagnosed officially with anxiety.

When I received this diagnosis, I was neither surprised nor upset. I knew what was coming, and I felt confident that I did the right thing. The lady that I was talking to suggested that I go speak to one of the doctors at the health center about some anxiety relief medicine, so I did. I am currently still on medicine today, and that is okay. It was also suggested that I go to some of the group therapy sessions that the program offered. I was willing, but I was a little nervous that we would all be in a circle singing kumbaya—meaning that I would feel awkward or weird sharing my experiences. When I got to the session, it was definitely not like that. We were all sitting at a big roundtable desk, and we were provided with worksheets and resources that would enable us to manage our anxiety or other mental health disorders. This group therapy helped me through my disorder, and allowed me to truly see the light at the end of the tunnel.

Throughout this experience, I learned a lot about having to manage anxiety. A lot of these tips will help you as well, no matter what you do or don't go through. Remember though that I am not your doctor or mental health specialist, I'm just here to share the information that helped me and that I pray will help you. I highly recommend seeking help for your situation. These specialists will not judge you; they will be extremely proud of you for asking for help. I remember the day I went and talked to the mental health specialist; she told me that she was proud of me for going to ask for help. I was extremely proud of myself because it takes a lot to ask for help sometimes, and also because I had to make myself go inside. I was fearful, so I literally stood still right outside the door before I went in to get help.

Exodus 14:14 NIV: "The Lord will fight for you; you need only to be still."[67]

---

67   Bible Gateway. (2019). Bible Gateway Passage: Exodus 14:14 – New International Version [online]

TIPS AND STRATEGIES[68]:

- Stay present. Stay focused; do not focus on what is happening an hour from now or weeks from now. Focus on the current moment. Do not stress about what is to come, because the Lord has already paved a way and He knows what you'll face.
- Breathe.
  - Breathing is the most essential thing to do. You have to breathe in order to survive, and one of the most important tips for someone suffering from anxiety or any mental health disorder is to breathe.
  - Breathe deeply. In and out, slowly. A lot of people suggest counting the number of breaths you take, but I personally find it a little more stressful to go about it that way. Instead, focus on breathing in and out slowly.
  - Focus on your breathing all of the time. A super common thing for me and many anxiety sufferers is that we will almost forget to breathe. Always make sure you are breathing, and if that is the only thing you can focus on, then focus on that.
- WebMD suggests the "3-3-3 rule":
  - Name three things you see.
  - Name three things you hear.
  - Move three parts of your body.
  - This will help bring you back to center and to focus. I call this the "grounding" rule.
- Write down what is going through your head.

---

68 Hughes, Locke. 2017. "How to Stop Feeling Anxious Right Now." WebMD. WebMD. March 2, 2017.

- I have done this numerous times in the private sections of my laptop, or in notes on my phone. I do this because it helps me clear my head. Sometimes that's all it truly takes—just letting it all out of your system.
- Pray about it.
  - The most obvious, yet most important one: Pray daily, even multiple times a day, that the Lord will heal you from your disorder and will allow you to find that peace.
- Set goals for yourself.[69]
  - If some days it's hard and challenging to get up and out of your bed in the morning, remind yourself that it is okay and that you are still strong and worthy. Set a goal to get up out of your bed by 11 each morning (for example).
  - Set goals for yourself to write more and to express your thoughts on paper—through art, writing, or anything else.
  - Set a goal for yourself to get twenty minutes of fresh air each day.
- Get physical.
  - It helps to get active and to try to set a routine for yourself.
  - It may be a little challenging to find the motivation for a workout multiple times a week, but set a goal for yourself to get outside and just walk around your backyard or down the street and back.
- Eat well.
  - Find and develop a good diet.

---

69 Griffin, R. Morgan. 2015. "10 Natural Depression Treatments." WebMD. WebMD. May 17, 2015.

- Find a diet plan or make meals that you know would really pick you up, allow you to work harder, and clear your mind.
- Sleep and rest.
  - Make sure you get plenty of sleep each night.
  - According to the National Sleep Foundation,[70] teenagers (ages 14-17) need eight to ten hours of sleep, young adults (18-25) need seven to nine hours, adults (26-64) need seven to nine hours, and older adults (65+) need seven to nine hours as well.
- Challenge yourself.
  - Challenge yourself to try new things, and to try things in which you have always been interested.
  - Challenge yourself to hang out with friends and to experience new and different social situations.
  - Challenge yourself daily.

I pray that all this helps you, and I hope you know that you will win this battle. You will; I have hope that you will. Just always remember that the Lord has placed these specialists and doctors in this world to be His hands and feet to help you through your journey. Always remember it is totally okay to ask for help. It is never something to feel ashamed of, especially not in this day and age where the stigma against mental health issues is lessening each day. Pray about your situation, and trust that the Lord will deliver you.

Always remember that the change begins with you. You can't change unless if you work to make it happen, so push through the hardships and grow with God. He will not

---

70 Sleep Foundation. "How Much Sleep Do We Really Need?"

leave you hanging, nor will He forsake you. He is right there with you in this journey. You need not fear, just pray. Everything will come around full circle and it will all be incredible. God is good and God will do the amazing through you.

END OF CHAPTER TAKEAWAYS:

While this is a more tactic-based chapter, it is healthy and good for reflection. I pray that you will use this as a time of closure and as a means for reflection as you move into this new season of help.

BIBLE VERSES:

- 2 Corinthians 3:17 NIV

QUESTIONS FOR REFLECTION:

- How are you going to use the suggestions above in your growth through your present situation, regardless of whether you deal with a mental health disorder or not?
- How can you help yourself by using these suggestions?
- What change do you hope to see when you challenge yourself to grow stronger?

ACTIONABLE TAKEAWAYS:

- Challenge yourself by applying these tips to your life, no matter what your situation looks like in the present.
- Keep a planner or bullet journal where you organize your day, your goals for the month or
- week, and your sleep schedule. It is very effective!

- I was inspired by my good friend Gavin Schrantz, who keeps the cutest bullet journal where she organizes everything.
- Pray about this growth and change, and how you want to see God work through it.

PRAYER:

Hey God. I am transitioning into a new season and phase in my life. On this journey, I pray that You will hold me close and allow me to keep my eyes on You. It is such an incredible thing to be on this journey to wellness, and I pray for accountability. Thank you, Father, for opening my eyes to my potential. Amen.

CHAPTER 21

TAKE UP YOUR CROSS

———

John 10:10 NIV: The thief comes only to steal and kill and destroy; I have come that they may have life, and have it to the full.[71]

You're staring the Devil in the face. You're staring anxiety, depression, trauma, etc. in the face. You see it mocking you, you see it ready to see what move you are going to make. It's ready to try to trick you into falsehood and the lies of himself—the Devil.

It's time to fight. It's time to cling to the Lord. It's time to be able to raise our hands, breathe in deeply, exhale, and know that we won. It's time to push the Devil away and to hold onto the progress we have made, and to further that progress. To not let the destroyer destroy. To not let the stealer steal.

———

71   Bible Gateway. (2019). Bible Gateway Passage: John 10:10 – New International Version [Online]

To know that we defeated the thing that is so common. To know that we put a brave face on, and went about our day in the strongest way possible. To know that we did everything we could to get through it, and we did it successfully. It's time to fight, but it's also time to win. It's time to release, but it's also time to withstand. It's time to feel. It's time to breathe.

Suffering from anxiety or any mental illness is truly a debilitating and exhausting thing. Sometimes we feel as though we lost that will to push through, and sometimes we feel as though we just aren't strong enough to do it. It's time to pick your head up, put your brave face on, and put your hand on your heart. It's time to breathe in deep and to look up, to realize what it is you're actually fighting for. It's time to remember that what you're fighting for is not only for protection and healing, but also for your own advantage to grow stronger. It's time to remember that you are fighting not only for yourself, but also for others. You are fighting to bring awareness, wisdom, and understanding to something so hard to understand.

You are fighting to defy the odds and to be a game changer. A leader. This is your fight, but it's also the Lord's and the Lord is with you always. He never leaves your side. He watches as the tides turn and roll in as the ship crashes safely onto shore, with you ready to defy the odds and prepare for battle. This moment. This moment is all you.

Joshua 1:9 NIV: Have I not commanded you? Be strong and courageous. Do not be afraid; do not be discouraged, for the Lord your God will be with you wherever you go."[72]

Picture this. You're standing in the middle of a busy city with thousands of people walking past you and nothing is going right. The taxi zoomed past you and you missed it. You're slowly running out of funds for the duration of your time there. You can't help but feel lost. You feel like you are standing in the middle ground, but you have no idea what's going on. You are anxious. You feel frightened. You start to feel numb. You feel afraid. What are you going to do? Are you going to take up your cross and move forward and accept the feelings you're feeling, or are you going to shrink to the ground and wallow in fear? What are you going to do?

Take up your cross. What exactly do I mean by taking up your cross? Well, Billy Graham once said that taking your cross means to put to death your plans and to accept and follow what the Lord has in mind for you instead. Essentially, what Billy Graham means is that Jesus called us to accept and follow Him and to commit our whole lives to Him, not just little portions of it, or whenever we feel it necessary. As Jesus said in Luke 9:23 NIV, "Then he said to them all: 'Whoever

---

72 Bible Gateway. (2019). Bible Gateway Passage: Joshua 1:9 – New Testament Version [Online]

wants to be my disciple must deny themselves and take up their cross daily and follow me.'"[73]

It is so important to follow the Lord and to do what He asks daily.

The reason I bring up how important it is to take up the cross, and to do so daily, is because one common thing that triggers anxiety in people is when things aren't going accordingly to plan. It causes individuals to become irritable and to become restless and unsure. I can definitely speak to that because that was one thing that triggered my anxiety from time to time, before I accepted and told myself that it's okay if things don't go accordingly to plan.

It's so important to let the Lord in and to let Him take your hand and lead you through this life. Years ago, I would make a plan for each day of the week in which I would wear T-shirts versus cute outfits. This never went accordingly to plan, due to laziness or just things that popped up in the week, and when it didn't go according to plan, sometimes I would feel weird or just a little anxious about that matter. Now, in present times, I know I have classes, and I know I'm going to talk to people at points in the day, but I no longer try to hold onto or run a specific deadline for when events can take place. I am this way now because I take up my cross and allow the Lord to carry out His plans in His perfect way. His plans are always better than ours are, anyway.

---

73 Bible Gateway. (2019). Bible Gateway Passage: Luke 9:23 – New Testament Version [Online]

I feel strongly about this fact right here: allow yourself to feel the feelings, specifically the physical feelings, that you're feeling. No matter how nasty or tough the feelings are, allow them to come in. Don't allow them to completely destroy you either physically or mentally, but don't try to bottle them up either. That is a very dangerous game to play because in the end, even if it's days later, you could have an even worse breakdown of sorts. Be very mindful of how you carry yourself and your feelings when you are in a rough spot emotionally.

Also remember that while sometimes you may be dealing with major depression and it is hard for you to get out of bed and do normal tasks each day, you still end up doing it even if it takes a long time. Thus, you are still winning this war. You are winning the fight. You are still one of the strongest people around, and you are still worthy. Never ever let anyone tell you otherwise. You are winning this war even if you do what to some is an easy task. You are winning this war no matter where you are in life. You are winning this war because you are choosing to put on a brave face, a smile, and lift your chin up. You are proving to others that you are capable and that you are ready.

No matter what you struggle with, always choose to take up your cross. Don't be afraid of change, because change is good. It's good to grow. Never let anyone tell you that you are unworthy or not strong enough, because you are truly worthy and very strong. You deserve to feel happy and you deserve to be at peace with yourself. Always try to better yourself because at the end of the day, the Lord wants your mind to be a safe place, not a battleground. Keep your head held high, and everything will be okay.

END OF CHAPTER TAKEAWAYS:

BIBLE VERSES:
- John 10:10 NIV
- Joshua 1:9 NIV

QUESTIONS FOR REFLECTION:
- When you think of taking up your cross, how does that look for you?
- How can you apply taking up your cross to your life?
- How has God worked through your life in a positive manner like no other?

ACTIONABLE TAKEAWAYS:
- Welcome change. Pray about it as it comes, but be open to change.
- Always remember that you have the Lord all around you and He won't leave you, even when times get really tough.
- Draw a picture of a cross with a bible verse that means a lot to you, and keep it close.

PRAYER:
Hey God. You are so amazing and good to me, and I am in awe of Your goodness. I am thankful that You sent Your son to die for me and my sins. I am thankful that I have the opportunity to experience Your grace and goodness. I pray that You will remind me daily of what You have done and what You will do. I also pray that You will keep my eyes focused forward. Amen.

CHAPTER 22

HIGHS AND LOWS

———

God is greater than my highs and lows. He knows all. He is greater. He is mightier. Everything bad that comes my way is going to pass. Everything that brings me happiness, fleeting or long-lasting, will still pass, but the memories will remain. Everything that has came my way and has almost destroyed me emotionally, is gone. They were fleeting moments too. God is greater than the highs and lows. He is always greater.

Romans 8:28 NIV: And we know that in all things God works for the good of those who love him, who have been called according to his purpose.[74]

In the Summer of 2019, I dealt with a lot. I dealt with a breakup that I initiated, a hostess job at a local Mexican

---

74 Bible Gateway. (2019). Bible Gateway Passage: Romans 8:28 – New Testament Version [Online]

restaurant that I loved, and an abundance of joy throughout it all. One of the biggest lows I dealt with was when I was manipulated and gaslighted by someone in my life. Briefly, I was in a toxic relationship, and he began verbally harming me. I began to feel worthless and trapped. After a lot of soul searching, I knew I had to walk away from our relationship before it destroyed me completely. I want those of you dealing with similar circumstances to know I understand your pain and you're not alone. If you have ever had a friend, family member, or lover who hurt you emotionally in ways that hurt so bad you have mental scars, it's a really hard thing to deal with. It was truly one of the lows at this time in my life.

The Lord gave me the strength to end things and cut off any means of connection with this person. It was so hard because I kept trying to find the good in him. I finally ended the relationship and I knew God was truly there every single minute. I knew that He would provide, and He sure did. That was something I'm very proud of, and I thank God for it every day.

While it was a major low to go through such a toxic relationship and all that came with it, it did teach me a lot, so that, to me, could be a high in some ways. Furthermore, God uses this low for me to run into His arms and to trust Him that He will pull me out of the difficult place. Guess what? He will do the exact same for you; you just need to let Him in.

It's such a blessing to know that the Lord is standing there with open arms waiting for us to run into them at any hour of the day. It's such a blessing to know that we are always welcome, and that we always have a true and safe home with Him. He is our Heavenly Father, and a great one He is. The

Lord is forever and always amazing, and the Lord is ready for us to come to Him with our highs and lows. He is ready to celebrate with us when we achieve that dream that He made happen, and He is ready to hold us while we are in tears because of a discouraging thing that happened. He is ready, and He is prepared.

The song "Highs and Lows" by Hillsong Young and Free really hits home and makes me think about this deeply. If you need to calm your heart, this one is for you. No matter how dark things are, God is running right beside you. He sees you as you walk through the dark night with sorrow in your mind and fear in your heart. He knows that you are fearful of His grace, because you feel you are undeserving. But fear not, God is right there. He wants to aid you and pull you up from your lows.

Joshua 1:9 NIV: Have I not commanded you? Be strong and courageous. Do not be afraid; do not be discouraged, for the Lord your God will be with you wherever you go.[75]

In these lows, it feels hard and almost impossible to recognize that your feelings are valid until you accept it. It is imperative that you understand that your feelings are valid: sadness or

75 Bible Gateway. (2019). Bible Gateway Passage: Joshua 1:9 – New Testament Version [Online]

depression, worry or anxiety, you name it, it is valid. My friend Abby Reinert shared how once she recognized that her feelings were valid, it allowed her to go get the help she needed.

Before Abby got help, she was battling with the fact that people may not understand her or may not think that her feelings need as much attention as they do. She also struggled with the doubt that since she comes from a good family, good town, goes to a great college, and more, that her feelings shouldn't be happening. Does that sound familiar? Fear not, you are not alone in this. Abby told me how she was able to overcome that fear, go to her parents, and explain her feelings and hurt to them.

That sounds kind of scary, right? Opening up to your loved ones about something that is genuinely hurting you? Well, her parents understood her and were proud of her for reaching out and getting the help she needed. She was able to find the encouragement she needed to fight her way through the hard times that threatened and the weight depression placed on her heart. Even after she received the help she needed and medication to help balance things out, she still noted that the spring semester of her sophomore year in college was tough. It was hard, but she began to notice and see the good things.

It didn't take long for her to realize how things were changing, and how this change was a good thing. Change doesn't have to always be scary; it can be exciting. Abby was, and still is, rewarded for her strength. She had courage to stand up for herself and ask for help when she needed it the most. She continues to ask for help when she is hurting, and that allows her to grow stronger. Through this process and time of change, she was able to grow closer to God. She would go to church on Sundays and she would absorb the content more instead of just halfway listening. Through God-given strength she is able to get up for classes and continue with her daily activities. Even during that low, the depression, she was still able to find a high: overall strength and peace from attending church each week.

Finally, Abby encourages everyone to go to a parent, a loved one, or someone super close to you when you are initially asking for help. When you have an onset of symptoms, don't wait, and reach out to someone in your immediate circle. Like I did, Abby talked to her parents. It can be anyone you want, but make sure you talk with someone you know will listen and will try to understand to the best of their ability. Never be afraid to reach out.

Be strong. Reach out. Ask for reassurance. Ask for assistance. Ask for a friend, even if all you do is sit on the couch while watching soap operas for hours on end. Do not be afraid. God has placed these people—family, friends, therapists, doctors, surgeons, counselors, etc.—on earth to be His hands and feet. To be the ones who save your life when you are in need of a major surgery. To be the ones who rescue you from yourself when you are at your wits' end. To be the ones who help you when you just need a friend or supporter. To be the ones who are there. To be His people, and to be the ones who keep you on track here on this earth.

The people in your life don't want to see you in these lows permanently. They want to see you grow, they want to see you move from the lows to the highs. They know what can be done, and they will aid you in finding that God-given treatment you may need, or just by providing a shoulder to cry on. Let these people in. They do not want to hurt you; they want to help you grow strong and be the person God designed you to be.

These people I speak of also include therapists. If things get to be too much, whether you fear you are struggling with anxiety or depression, or maybe the stress of school or work is too much, I encourage you to take advantage of therapy. I especially encourage this for college students, because therapy is free (covered by tuition) for students at most universities and colleges. Make yourself aware of these resources, wherever they are: at your school, college, workplace, or town. These people want to help you. They see you when you are at your highs, and they see you when you are at your lows. Everyone around you will respect and honor you for stepping out and pursuing the help and treatment that you may need. They will never look down on you for doing so, so let go of that fear and start chasing the highs rather than the lows.

1 John 4:4 NIV: You, dear children, are from God and have overcome them, because the one who is in you is greater than the one who is in the world.[76]

76 Bible Gateway. (2019). Bible Gateway Passage: 1 John 4:4 – New Testament Version [Online]

God will never let you go, and He is too good to do so. He loves us all for our hearts, and He wouldn't leave us just because of one little issue. He has overcome it all. All of our highs, all of our lows. All of our hardships, all of our triumphs. We are called to continue and to put our best foot forward, and to trust that He will use us even in our lows to build His kingdom and share His good name.

The Lord will not look at you differently because of a past mistake. He already knew it was happening, and He knew when it was going to happen. He knows your story, and He knows what you are going through. He knows that you have been going through a lot of pain and suffering. He wants you to know that He loves you endlessly, no matter what happens. He has paved a way for you previously, currently, and will continue to do so in the future. Don't give up now, and stay true to yourself. Trust in the Lord's promises for your life, because He is with you no matter what. He is always there.

No battle is any match for our God. That depression is no match, nor is that doubt and fear of people not understanding. Those sleepless nights are no match for God. You are worthy, and you will see a high soon.

After having a time of lows, you are guaranteed to have some highs. Pay attention to the little things as you walk through life; they could be more impactful than you could ever imagine. Just never forget that Jesus died on that cross on that dark day for us. He knew all of the mistakes we would make; He knew the fear and doubt we would have, but He still chose to love us and die for us. His Father, our Heavenly Father, sent Him, His only son, to die for us. Those of us who suffer, those of us who celebrate. Those of us who have stress, anxiety, depression, PTSD, or any other condition, physical or mental. He died for YOU.

He whose love is so great has died for you. Rest easy in that truth and know that He will always pull you from those lows and allow your faith to grow tremendously. Continue to reach out just like Abby Reinhart did, and never be afraid of judgement. You are worthy and amazing in every way.

Finally, remember that He truly does love you even when you are in your lows. His love and grace are abundant, and they never fail, nor do they ever cease. God is faithful, and He won't let you go.

END OF CHAPTER TAKEAWAYS:

BIBLE VERSES:
- Romans 8:28 NIV
- Joshua 1:9 NIV
- 1 John 4:4 NIV

QUESTIONS FOR REFLECTION:
- When you are at your highs, do you ever feel yourself being attacked by the Devil? How does this feel, and what do you do, or can you do, to allow yourself to stand firm in your faith?
- When you are at your lows, what do you tend to do to help yourself?
- When you think about how God loves you at both your highs and lows, what does this feel like?

ACTIONABLE TAKEAWAYS:

- Draw a picture of a mountain. Do you see how there are peaks and there are valleys? Remember, God can move mountains.
- Make a point to look up the resources that are available in your community with regard to mental health. Mental health is important to take care of even if you don't have a diagnosed disorder.
- Seek treatment if deemed necessary.

PRAYER:

Heavenly Father, I thank You for both my highs and lows. I thank You for bringing me through the worst of it, and for showing me that it all is okay. I thank You for being the foundation and the One who I can always count on. No low can compare to Your might. Thank you, Father. Amen.

CHAPTER 23

UNCOMFORTABLE

Do you ever feel uneasy for no apparent reason? That hollowness within your stomach? That pit in your heart that threatens to deepen? Those butterflies within your tummy that threaten to escape? That rage in your mind when things just don't add up or make sense can make you uncomfortable.

Feeling uncomfortable is oftentimes prominent when the Lord is working in our lives. We may know there is about to be a shift in our lives, but we may not believe it or understand it at the time.

Right now, while writing this chapter, I somewhat feel that way because this book is in the works and my life is about to change during and after publication. Don't get me wrong, I am extremely excited, but I am also nervous about it at the same time. It is a lot of pressure on my shoulders knowing that this book is going to be published, but it is also extremely exciting because I have so much to share with the world. It makes me feel uncomfortable, in a good way, to know that people are going to know my heart so deeply.

This uncomfortable feeling will propel you to chase your dreams just like I am doing. This is the feeling that will change your life forever, once the discomfort is gone, because you will realize your blessing and miracle. You may feel this way due to anticipation, fear, stress, hope, sadness, worry, doubt, excitement, or a combination of all of those things. For me, in this present moment, that's what it is: everything!

I am currently starting a brand-new chapter in my life. The chapter is unknown, but I have faith that God will use it in the best way possible. To see my dream come to fruition is making me slightly uncomfortable, but in the best way possible. To think about what is coming in my life is providing lots of hope too. I pray that you will never forget or lose hope about what the Lord can and will do in your life. He promises so many incredible things, and He will deliver. He will shine that light and push you through it all. No season or moment of being uncomfortable can or will hinder the promise that Jesus has for your life.

What happens when you start questioning it, though? When this uncomfortable feeling leaves you absolutely restless and out of it? Anxious? Depressed? All of it? What happens then?

Luke 5:22 NIV: Jesus knew what they were thinking and asked, "Why are you thinking these things in your hearts?"[77]

---

[77] Bible Gateway. (2019). Bible Gateway Passage: Luke 5:22 – New Testament Version [Online]

As mentioned in Luke 5:22, Jesus asked his people, "why do you question your hearts?" He knows that they are human and will feel emotions, but He questions them when they question their hearts asking if what is right is actually wrong, or if what is wrong is actually right; meaning, the questioning that goes along with being uncomfortable. You know what I'm talking about; you know what Jesus is talking about. It is feeling unsure when you know that the truth is that a way will be paved and you will be okay, but then having that somehow flip into, "but I don't know, God … I just don't know."

What happens then? Why are we put into these uncomfortable situations? One answer: to allow us to grow in our walk with Christ. The utmost important thing that we could do in our lives is to grow closer in our walk with Him. This is because He has done, and will continue to do, so many incredible things. He will work in our lives even when we are incredibly uncomfortable or disheartened.

What does God want us to do? He wants us to be positive and to trust in Him and His glory.

Psalm 56:3 NIV: When I am afraid, I put my trust in you.[78]

78 Bible Gateway. (2019). Bible Gateway Passage: Psalm 56:3 – New Testament Version [Online]

One thing about being uncomfortable is it's important to think positively about your situation. "What would Jesus do?" This is the slogan that is found on so many bracelets (of which I'm a proud owner), stickers, and many other keepsakes. This slogan holds so much truth and wonder, but it also provides some comfort to think about what Jesus would do in a given situation. The healer. The victor. The winner. He would choose to love. He would love others. He would love the situation in His own incredible way. He would pray to His Father and ask what to do.

This is the perfect reminder for us during these times because it's easy to become irritable or hostile as we await what's to come. It's very easy to do that, but what's important for us during this season of waiting is to love others just like Jesus does. It's essential that we still spread His grace and love, and trust Him in every second. It is so important to love others and to show them His grace, as that will continue to build the Kingdom. That could be an essential part of the waiting process as well.

Remember, during these seasons of discomfort, we bear the most fruit. The fruits of the spirit are incredibly important in our walk with Christ.

Galatians 5:22-23 NIV: But the fruit of the Spirit is love, joy, peace, forbearance, kindness, goodness, faithfulness,

gentleness and self-control. Against such
things there is no law.[79]

The reason I am dropping those fruits of the Spirit in is
because, like my Uncle Harold says, once the Holy Spirit is
allowed into our hearts, our lives will truly change forever.
Don't you notice that the fruits of the Spirit are all positive
and healthy things? Nothing scary. Nothing harmful. It is
all goodness. That is where Jesus wants you to be all of the
time. Not just in your season of discomfort, but also in your
season of waiting that is causing you to be uncomfortable.
He wants to witness you bear the fruits of the Spirit that
He has sought out for your heart to receive.

No matter what your present situation may look like, you will
make it through. The discomfort and unease are no match
for our God.

You are never alone. While you are uncomfortable during
your season of waiting, it is very easy to get anxious and
to worry about things that come your way. It is easy to be
anxious about things that aren't even worth focusing on.
It is easy to fall off the sidewalk during your walk in this
season of discomfort, too. You are not alone, though.

The Lord is watching you; the Lord is holding you during
this time. He is right there with you and He is preparing you
for your blessing. He is preparing you for the miracle that is

79 Bible Gateway. (2019). Bible Gateway Passage: Galatians 5:22-23 –
    New Testament Version [Online]

due to come soon. He knows exactly when, where and how this miracle will happen. He is just waiting for you to pray to Him and give Him the discomfort you have felt for quite some time. He needs you to release this to Him, trust Him, pray a lot, and be as patient as possible.

It is also easy for us to feel uncomfortable during our seasons of waiting if we are waiting for a relationship. My friend Jason Blackwell gave me some important wisdom about waiting, trust, and relationships: "Something I've learned is that me not trusting someone with that is really me not trusting God. If He has given me peace about being in a relationship with someone, I should trust that I am right where I am supposed to be and put forth everything into that situation that He has blessed me with." This advice really made me think because I do struggle with jealousy and just a pure feeling of uncomfortableness around trusting guys, but it's so important that we trust God first. Once we trust God, that season and feeling of discomfort will relieve itself and eventually we will be able to trust everyone.

People are not here to hurt us. They actually want to see us do well in life, and they want to be our supporters throughout. There will be people that cross your path that end up hurting you, but know that you still need to trust God first. As mentioned above, once you trust in Him, everything else will fall into line. It will all work out and be okay.

Proverbs 3:5 NIV: Trust in the Lord with all your heart
and lean not on your own understanding[80]

Your path will continue to be made straight and in due time. Just trust and know that the Lord is good and that He will help and relieve you of your discomfort. You will find your place and you will know exactly what is going on when it happens. You will know when the blessing is coming. Trust that this discomfort will provide and allow for something super special and amazing to come to fruition. The Lord is holding your hand every step of the way—just trust in Him and give your battles to Him.

As Proverbs 3:5 ESV says, we are called to trust Him no matter what we go through. Do not fall into your own thoughts. Do not allow yourself to succumb to thoughts of fear and do not let your thoughts break your heart. This is much easier said than done, but as you bear the fruits of the spirit and gain wisdom on how to fight these battles, it will be easier. The mind is a very dangerous place sometimes, so allow the Lord to fill your mind with grace, peace, and hope. The Lord will provide so much, everything will work out, and you will be even stronger. The Lord doesn't want your mind or heart to be a battleground; He wants it to be a safe place.

Finally, trust Him.

---

80 Bible Gateway. (2019). Bible Gateway Passage: Proverbs 3:5 – New Testament Version [Online]

END OF CHAPTER TAKEAWAYS:

BIBLE VERSES:

- Luke 5:22 NIV
- Psalm 56:3 NIV
- Galatians 5:22-23 NIV
- Proverbs 3:5 NIV

QUESTIONS FOR REFLECTION:

- When you are in a season of discomfort, what do you do first? How do you challenge that discomfort, or do you wait for it to pass?
- What can you do the next time you feel that uneasiness in your gut? How are you going to manage it?
- How are you going to let God work in your uncomfortableness?

ACTIONABLE TAKEAWAYS:

- When that feeling of discomfort arises, write down exactly what you're feeling and exactly what's going on in that present moment of your life.
- Remember that the present discomfort is not something that will always be present.
- Instead of running away from the discomfort, dive into it. Actively seek what is causing that discomfort, and work through the issues in your life that could be causing it.
- Stay in prayer about it.

PRAYER:

Hey God. I'm in a season of major discomfort, and I need all of the help I can get. I pray that You will continue to use me in this season even though I have no idea where to run. I pray that you will allow me to trust in You fully, and to see the good that inevitably will come from this. You are good. Amen.

CHAPTER 24

PAIN ... THEN VICTORY

———

Here we are. How does it feel to know that at the end of the day, despite the pain, there is still light? An overwhelming, powerful, and amazing light. How does it feel to know that God sent His one and only Son to die for our sins, and He is the ultimate healer and the One who saved us all? It truly is an amazing thing when we realize and truthfully believe that we have victory through Christ. We have victory through Him and because of Him. He died for our sins, and saved us from ourselves.

We suffered. We came. We saw. We listened. We heard. We have achieved victory. We have fought through some of the hardest times in our lives, gone through some pain that was undeniably hard and terrifying, but we made it through to the other side. Pain is something that will happen in our life no matter what. It is, without a doubt, discouraging, but it is up to us to find the positives from it. It is essential that we remember who came before us and died for our sins. Jesus Christ went through so much pain on the cross that day. He suffered, but He suffered with the knowledge that all of His people would be saved, freed, and would be in a much better state. He went through so much pain when He was nailed to the cross on that gloomy day, but He has the ultimate victory.

The Lord truly paid the ultimate price to save us, and to deliver us from the darkness that threatens. This is something we should be forever thankful for and keep in our hearts forevermore. But what happens when we just can't? I personally hate saying "I can't," but sometimes it is just that. We may be physically or mentally unable at the moment to do something. What then?

John 11:35 NIV: Jesus wept.[81]

Well, the first thing we can do is claim similarity and commonality with Jesus. Jesus did cry. It's so common for people to "forget" (because we don't literally forget; it just is overrun with our thoughts of His power and might) that Jesus actually was human too. He cried, he pleaded, he hurt: the same as us. Doesn't that make you feel better in a way? To know and believe that our own Savior felt emotional pain like we do? It seems very complex because we know Him as a perfect individual who was sent by his Father to come here and save us all, but yes, Jesus actually did feel human emotions, because He was human.

When He was nailed to that cross that day—the darkest day of all—he experienced pain like no other. Physical pain. The

---

81 Bible Gateway. (2019) *Bible Gateway Passage: John 11:35 – New International Version [online]*

nails that went in his wrists and ankles, the staring from the Romans as they looked at Him, and the crying from His people. He cried ... but He knew that God had a plan bigger than anything. Bigger than those nails going through Him, bigger than the Roman guards who believed they were so tough, bigger than the fears of doom that were coming from His supporters. He knew. He knows. He knows all.

And He knows that you will be okay.

He knows that you will make it through.

He knows that He will be right there next to you no matter what path you take, and no matter how far away you are.

Jesus claims the ultimate victory, and that is something worth celebrating. Through the hardship, blood, pain, and evangelizing, He found that victory and claimed it for himself and all of mankind.

A song that I love more than you could know is "See A Victory" by Elevation Worship. Throughout this song, we hear the message of how we know who He is and how we know that He is good. We know how He can change our lives forevermore and that a victory is in our destiny.

Even though we are in that state of fear, we won't back down. We won't quit our good fight just because of the hardships, and we won't back down from the giants that threaten.

Depression is no match for our God. Anxiety is no match for our God. PTSD is no match for our God.

We are capable. The Lord will see us through.

1 John 5:4 NIV: For everyone born of God overcomes the world. This is the victory that has overcome the world, even our faith.[82]

I have had the privilege of learning a lot from my good friend from high school, Connor Watson. Connor has been a great influence in my life, and he has a huge heart for serving others and for Jesus. One thing I never knew was his personal battle with depression. He describes it as this, and I think we can really take something from this message:

"I've struggled with depression. It's better than it was but it still hits me every now and then. Usually, I would have this complete disinterest and lack of motivation for doing anything. I would just hide away somewhere and I always had this terrible feeling that nobody really liked me and that I was on my own. For a while, this was detrimental in itself, because I was really making myself more lonely by telling myself this. I opened up eventually to my amazing girlfriend Hannah, who has been my constant companion for almost four years now. The other person was my mom, who has been a real rock for me throughout my life. Talking things

---

82   Bible Gateway. (2019). Bible Gateway Passage: 1 John 5:4 – New International Version [online]

through with them helped me a lot, and I still find that when depression hits, that's the way out."

It's incredible to see how both Connor's girlfriend, Hannah Russell, and his mom have helped him tremendously throughout his struggle. It shows how God sent Hannah into his life and proclaimed his mom to be his mother as a way to be His hands and feet and speak to Connor through these times. We can really learn from Connor in that it is important for us to seek that community, like Maci Bolin suggested earlier in this book. It is so important as believers to find those people who can understand us and who are always available to listen, and who know us for who we are.

Connor learned his method to working through his depression: "Talking things through with them helped me a lot, and I still find that when depression hits, that's the way out." Y'all, if you're looking for an answer on how to manage your depression, this is it. Pray that God will open your eyes and heart and bring someone into your life who can really help with your struggles. Whether that be depression, anxiety, another mental health disorder, or just regular stress, find that person. Talking it out can be a very helpful way to work through things, as it is a true way to "ground" yourself—bring yourself back down to earth when your head is in the clouds—and to really find that comfort and peace. It is imperative to bring people close to you while you are going through a difficult walk. They don't have to always understand the battle or exactly what you're dealing with, but as long as they try and as long as they listen, then that's more than anyone can ask for.

Jesus is always there too. Some days, I will just have a good ole' chat with Jesus when I am driving back from somewhere. It always gives me a sense of peace and comfort to know that my drives are times I dedicate to spending with Him.

If you're in a transition period in your life, Connor also offered some handy advice on how he manages stress: "Take a step back. Really take everything in and grasp what is going on. This will let you realize what things are important. It is really easy for things to stack up and weigh on you when, really, a lot of those things may not matter at all. Find time to enjoy yourself. Whatever it is that you like to do, do it. You can't spend your whole life working; sometimes you need to breathe." The part that stuck out to me from what Connor said is, "a lot of those things may not matter at all." Y'all, this is true!

Ask yourself this, will this matter three months from now? How about three years from now? You may just have your answer there. Take time to breathe and take time to reassure yourself during this hardship. You are still worthy and amazing, no matter what your GPA or class standing is, where your acceptances are coming from, or what causes worry. You are still worthy.

God calls us as believers to really pour into others and to love one another. This life is so complex and full of hardship at points that we feel like we are drowning. It is so important to celebrate the victories of others. Even if your friend texts you and says, "Guess what? I just got out of bed today and I made my bed up!" then celebrate that. Everything is worth celebration. Sometimes we get so caught up in life that we forget that we are doing things that we once thought were hard.

Celebrate yourself today and every day, but make sure you celebrate Jesus—the victor of the highest victory imaginable.

END OF CHAPTER TAKEAWAYS:

BIBLE VERSES:
- John 11:35 NIV
- 1 John 5:4 NIV

QUESTIONS FOR TAKEAWAYS:
- What victories have you experienced recently in life, and how did you celebrate those?
- How will you celebrate future victories?

ACTIONABLE TAKEAWAYS:
- Whenever you celebrate a victory, make a point to celebrate God through the victory, and remember Him for what He has done and what He will continue to do.
- Write down your victories. Whether it is a major victory or just something small, write them down. Look back on those victories in your darkest days.

PRAYER:
Heavenly Father, I am thankful for You. Your victory is the greatest of all, and I treasure that. You're so incredible in Your might and in all that you do. Thank you, and I am excited to see what You have in store for me next. Amen.

CHAPTER 25

THE BROKEN ONES

———

Broken. Shattered. Dismantled. Disheartened. Messy. Rough around the edges.

We are the broken ones. Only when we come to Jesus are we made whole again.

Psalm 34:18 NIV: The Lord is close to the
brokenhearted
and saves those who are crushed in spirit.[83]

To me, being broken means not having quite "enough." What is enough? That's the question that goes through our heads. It could mean not having enough attention, love, or support. It could be just feeling like you are not enough. It could be not being fully able to get that extra dose of "enough" from things here on earth.

———

83 Bible Gateway. (2019). Bible Gateway Passage: Psalm 34:18 – New International Version [online]

We aren't fully whole as is because there is something, and someone, missing. That's where our Lord steps in. He is the one we need, and His goodness is the something we need. He lives among us; He lives in our hearts and minds. He wants to know us. He wants to fill that ever-present void in our lives.

Think about being cracked. Visualize yourself and imagine your body being cracked all over in various locations. In some spots, the cracks run deeper, while other cracks are barely scratches, but still present. There are some cracks that are old—they formed a long time ago. There are some cracks that just developed yesterday.

While thinking about those cracks, no matter how big, small, old, or new, think about the Lord filling those cracks, like potholes in the pavement and cracks in the road in South Carolina. Think about the Lord renewing us. Think about how the Lord is filling those cracks. Those cracks could be anxiety. They could be an attempted but failed suicide. They could be the death of a lover, a family member, a friend, or an acquaintance. They could be depression. They could be doubt within your relationship. They could be that injury that impacted your life forever. They could be cancer. They could be the fear that you are unworthy. The Lord fills those cracks and voids. He is the one who is the superglue to our crack. The mend to our wound. The hope to our doubt. The filler to our void.

He is close to you. He sees your wounds; in fact He sees them all over you, whether they are physical or mental. He sees us in the present moment; every waking moment He is there. He sees you standing on the side of the street at midnight yelling at Him, asking Him why you are broken. He sees you drying your tears on a Monday morning after the scariest news came your way. He sees you in your brokenness, but He still uses you.

The thing is, we are chosen. We are the chosen ones, the loved ones. We are the broken ones that God chose to be broken but to be filled back up by His sweet and loving grace and kindness. We are chosen. You are chosen. Even when you feel like you are not, when you feel as though you are lacking, you are still worthy and chosen.

Jeremiah 1:5 NIV: "Before I formed you in the womb I knew you, before you were born I set you apart; I appointed you as a prophet to the nations."[84]

He knows us by name. He saw us before we were even embryos in our mothers' wombs. He mended our hearts together in just the way He designed, but things of this world got in our hearts once we stepped foot on the earth. This world caused some brokenness, but it caused us to be able to use this brokenness to build His kingdom, to be a prophet to the nations. To spread His goodness, that while we may be suffering, we are still chosen.

---

84 Bible Gateway. (2019). Bible Gateway Passage: Jeremiah 1:5 – New International Version [online]

He has such an incredible, powerful, and mighty plan for our lives. Each time we go down to our low point, whether that be in anxiety or plain irritability, or even when we are at the lowest point of our lives, He builds us back up and allows us to go in and use that story of healing and faith to prophecy to the nations and to spread His good works.

At the end of the day, it's just you and the Lord. Let that sink in, friends. At the end of the day, it is just you and the Lord. That day when you arrive at the gates of Heaven, it's just going to be you and the Lord. No one else. Just you and Him.

You will stand face to face with the One who has been by your side this whole time. The One who saved you from anxiety, depression, a suicide attempt, cancer, sicknesses, failed relationships, people leaving, etc. The One who loves you no matter what. While we're here on earth, remember that nobody can stop God's goodness in your life. He will continue to work through you always, despite you being broken, despite you being helpless and at times hopeless.

He will continue to work through you in ways that will aid others. For me, I use my anxiety as a format and platform for this book. For someone else, this could look like using their cancer diagnosis and then remission as a means of hope for other cancer patients. You don't have to let your brokenness be a dead end for you.

People will hurt you; they will forsake you; they will leave you; they will judge you. The Lord will not. The Lord never does. You may feel as though He is silent, but in your brokenness, remember this is an opportunity for you to change your perspective and to flip the flow, as Pastor Steven Furtick would say.

1 Peter 2:16 NIV: Live as free people, but do not use your freedom as a cover-up for evil; live as God's slaves.[85]

Despite being broken, but raised to freedom, we are called to serve. We are called to love. We are called to love one another no matter what. We are called to serve one another by lending a helping hand in times of darkness, by helping others when they are stuck in trouble, by being a friend, by sharing the Word, and by just being an all-around good person. It is so important to continue to serve.

The Lord fills up our brokenness, because while we are not whole on earth, we are whole in Christ. While the Lord fills up our brokenness, He also uses our brokenness. He uses it so we can share our testimonies and help people along the way. He uses it to allow us to grow and to see the other side of things. The Lord is forever good in this regard, and He will use you no matter where you are in your walk with Him and no matter where you are in life.

The Lord has fought for us despite us being the broken ones. If you truly love someone, you will fight for them. We are called to live like Jesus, so if you love someone, fight for them.

---

85 Bible Gateway. (2019). Bible Gateway Passage: 1 Peter 2:16 – New International Version [online]

If you truly love someone, it is important to work with them and try to support them despite their flaws or questionable actions. It is important to talk to them in a manner that shows you care. If you truly love someone, you will love them no matter what. No matter the things they do, no matter the grades they get, no matter the mistakes they make, no matter the hurt they cause, no matter the choices they make. If you truly love someone, you will work to help them get closer to Jesus. You will help them throughout their issues, their lows, and their highs.

This is called unconditional love and it describes how Jesus loves us. Meaning that there is no set time when He will stop loving us and giving us grace and peace. He loves us with no limits, just because he chooses to. Always choose to love like Jesus.

The world today needs all of the broken people (and trust me, we're all broken) to step it up, step forward, come together, and be the difference. I am tired of seeing people slow down past a wreck and then notice that no one else is helping them or at least checking in to see if they're okay. I am tired of seeing kids sit by themselves at lunch in the cafeteria because they don't know anyone else and no one is being nice to them. It is time for us to build that middle ground and to come together as a team of believers, to work together and create something super amazing.

While we are the broken ones, we are unstoppable. Our past can't dictate our future, and it can't hinder us from going for our goals. We are called to be the game changers and to be the ones who really make a difference in the lives of others.

Our brokenness and every void within are filled thanks to the Lord's grace. While we aren't perfect, we are perfect in Christ's eyes because, remember, He made us in His perfect image.

END OF CHAPTER TAKEAWAYS:

BIBLE VERSES:
- Psalms 34:18 NIV
- Jeremiah 1:5 NIV
- 1 Peter 2:16 NIV

QUESTIONS FOR REFLECTION:
- What are factors of your brokenness?
- How do you let God use your brokenness?
- How can and will you help others and yourself by sharing your story?

ACTIONABLE TAKEAWAYS:
- Find one way that you could use your story to impact others.
- Find one Bible verse that is useful, especially in your hard seasons, and memorize it to recite in times of need.

PRAYER:
Hey God. I am standing before you tonight, and I am humbled to be doing so. I am standing here in the midst of all of my brokenness and I'm asking you to shine a light on it and how I should use it. Allow me to remember that being broken is normal, and I will find the light. Amen.

CHAPTER 26

HEAVEN

———

Revelation 21:3 NIV: And I heard a loud voice from the throne saying, "Look! God's dwelling place is now among the people, and He will dwell with them. They will be his people, and God himself will be with them and be their God.[86]

Isn't it comforting to know that we have a Home that is without pain, that is a completely safe place, where we will be reunited with our loved ones, and where we will get to run into our Savior's arms? To know that there is a place that is without pain, anxiety, depression, stress, or sadness is very comforting. Isn't it also comforting to know that we get a little bit of a taste of Heaven while we are here on Earth?

---

86 Bible Gateway. (2019). Bible Gateway Passage: Revelation 21:3 –
New International Version [online]

Meaning, when we follow God and experience that fullness, the old things begin to wash away.

Throughout our life here on earth, it is important that we seek to know Him, and to know His voice. It is important that we strive to learn more about Him. It is also important to remember that the kingdom of Heaven is living within us. What a wonderful and powerful concept to think about! It is true, because once we accept Jesus Christ into our hearts, we have that peace and comfort that is from Heaven, thanks to Jesus.

As I said before, Heaven is definitely a location, but it is also something in our hearts. It is something that is deep within us and something that really pulls us. Heaven is something that causes our heart to stir, sometimes by just hearing the word. Thinking about Heaven brings me great peace, and it brings me even greater peace to know and hold true to the promise that Heaven is among and within us. It also brings me great peace to know that our loved ones and beloved furry friends will also be up there welcoming us Home.

My friend Abby Cowan from my sorority shared a song that hit home for me. The song is "Heaven" by Passion. This song just makes me think, but it also brings me great peace. I am so in awe of the fact that we serve such a great King who would allow for such amazing miracles to occur—one of them, by far the most important, being Heaven. I highly recommend listening to it, because it provides such an empowering visual for what Heaven is.

In this song, we get the sense of the absolute dire need we have as Christians to truly know Him and to know His goodness. We find that we will do anything to get to know Him better. It provides an interesting and distinct visual for me. It makes me think about how important it is that we try to get as close to Jesus and try to really know Him as well as we can. It is so important to get to know His heart. It is so important that we do so to really know Him and who He is, and also that we'll know and feel more about the Heaven that is within us.

It is also important to know that we have the breath of Heaven within us. The same breath allowed Jesus to work so many miracles not only with us today but also when he brought Lazarus back to life and when he turned water into wine many years ago. It is so powerful to think about how we have that hope and light living directly within us, and to know that Jesus continues to pour into us daily.

It is so easy when we are anxious and everything in our lives feels like it's falling apart in some way to not remember the promises that are in store for us. To not remember the miracles that came before us, and to not remember that those same or similar miracles can happen for us. During the trials we face every day in our lives, it is imperative to turn toward the Lord and to remember that He is here for us and that He wants to help us grow. He wants us to trust in Him that He can rock our world just like he did when Moses was attempting to cross the Red Sea, and God in turn parted it so he could walk through. It's important to remember how a blind man was able to see, all by the grace of God. These miracles can also happen to you, and so they will.

Colossians 3:2 NIV: Set your minds on things above, not on earthly things.[87]

Heaven is within us, God is beside us, and Jesus is our Savior, so who do we really have to fear? No one. It's time to come home to the Lord and to fall into His arms. It's time to trust in Him and to know that while life is crazy sometimes, the Lord will allow you to grow and He will continue to bring that perfect peace into your life. God is forever good for how He comes and pulls us from the shadows into a healthy spot and breathes life back into us.

Sometimes, after I have a pretty large run-in with anxiety, I feel like hope and happiness have been sucked out of me. There was one night very recently when this happened. I was working on writing this book and I began to get increasingly anxious as I thought about all of the homework and writing I had to do by that Monday. I felt myself growing even more restless and my hope diminishing. It really felt like I was being poked by a thorn in my side.

During this moment, I realized that I needed support and help. A friend of mine, Jonathon Rhymer, told me that I needed to cut some unimportant things out of my life and really manage my time well. He told me it is important to remember that it will be okay soon and that everything will work out accordingly. I took that advice and I felt so much better when I began to prioritize things. I was fully able to

---

87 Bible Gateway. (2019). Bible Gateway Passage: Colossians 3:2 – New International Version [online]

focus on the things that really had to get done, and to focus on the things that are more time-sensitive.

That night, I began cutting things out of my to-do list. It sounds silly because these are things you think you need to do, but how badly do you really need to do them right now? It obviously differs for whatever thing it may be, and definitely keep up with your work, but for anyone who suffers from anxiety or stress, this is for you. It seems like such an obvious thing to do, especially when you're in college, but once things start adding up on your plate it begins to get a little difficult. Take a step back and prioritize your life.

Once I began cutting things that really weren't essential or necessary, I began to feel my joy return. I felt that peace and I had that knowledge that I needed to succeed and push forward. All by the grace of God, I felt Him breathe that life back into me, and I felt myself getting back to normal.

Y'all, while that may not be some massive miracle, it was still a very important moment in my life in which I felt at peace from anxiety and received wisdom that helped me go forth in life. It is still a miracle because I do suffer from a diagnosed mental disorder and to feel that heavenly peace fill my lungs again and cast out all of the worry was such a blessing. God is so good, without a doubt, and I am very thankful for the ability to cling to Him no matter what happens.

Remember, Heaven is in your heart and you have the breath of Heaven instilled in you. Don't forget that while things get hectic, tides turn, and the ship threatens to buckle and break, you will make it. Focus on God and things above, just like

Colossians 3:2 mentions. Always remember this even when you are in your darkest moments. God will rescue you as always and bring you to the light.

END OF CHAPTER TAKEAWAYS:

BIBLE VERSES:
- Revelations 21:3 NIV
- Colossians 3:2 NIV

QUESTIONS FOR REFLECTION:
- When you think of Heaven, what comes to mind for you?
- When you read Colossians 3:2, isn't it powerful to hear how God tells us to focus on things above, rather than the earthly things?
- What is a major takeaway for you with regard to Heaven?

ACTIONABLE TAKEAWAYS:
- Write down all of the things that come to mind when you think of Heaven. Whenever you get anxious, stressed, sad, lonely, etc., look at this list and revert your mind back to the Heavenly and positive things above.

PRAYER:
Father, I am thankful. I am thankful that you have provided a home on this earth, as well as Home in Heaven. I am thankful that you have provided such an abundant amount of peace that transpires over all of the fear in our hearts. Allow me to see the good and the positive in all things, even when I am hurting. I am thankful. Amen.

CHAPTER 27

SNAPCHAT MEMORIES

———

Every day I wake up in the morning knowing that I will see a new Snapchat memory from the year or even from years before. It always makes me nostalgic and brings up some sad feelings, because of good times that have passed and happy feelings of those good times that I am thankful to have had. I always see cute pictures of my beloved dog, Tucker—my ride-or-die, my sidekick, my love bug, and my best friend—and sometimes I see things that aren't as enjoyable.

There was one morning in particular, not too long ago at all, where I saw a memory that made me realize how much of a stronghold anxiety once had on my life. In early August 2018, I suffered from extreme headaches in the mornings. I would deal with slight tingles in my hands and face, and I would feel myself growing more and more anxious. Some of those mornings I would remember dreams I had had that could have triggered something within me to cause me to be anxious. The pain was unpleasant beyond words, and it made me very confused. I had no idea why my body was retaliating against me in this manner.

I remember hearing God telling me that it was anxiety, and so I began to pray; this had been heavy on my heart for not just the hours I dealt with the headaches, but for a few weeks at this point. Not a lot of time went by before I was diagnosed with Generalized Anxiety Disorder and I was medicated for it. I rarely have those headaches anymore, which just shows the true blessing of anxiety medication. It was that "tell-tale" moment that really got me thinking, and it made me aware that this condition wasn't just some mental health issue that impacts your thought process; it impacts your body as well.

I am no doctor, but luckily we have great health professionals out there who can fully explain this. Harvard Health Medical Center explains how anxiety develops and the anatomy behind it. We learn from the Harvard Medical Center that the feeling rises into the amygdala, the region of the brain where emotion is intensely processed, and the thought moves on to the sympathetic nervous system. Upon reaching this nervous system, it triggers responses such as an increased heart rate, tingling, changes in breathing rate, and inadequate blood flow to the brain. That sounds purely terrifying, doesn't it? Now, I agree. That doesn't sound pretty, and it definitely isn't pretty when you are suffering from a major anxiety-induced headache or any physical anxiety symptom. However, that is what medicine is for and that is why we should be grateful to have it.

Personally, I am grateful to be on medication for my anxiety disorder. It has allowed me to feel like my brain is actually working properly when I am in those high-anxiety, stress – or pressure-filled states. The key component to this whole thing is that you need to talk with a doctor to decide if medication is for you. It is definitely for some people, but for others it is not. There are always other alternatives. God has given us these doctors, therapists, and everyone around us to pour His grace and love into us, to be His hands and feet, and to help us through the hardest times in our lives. It is up to us and God, and His plan for us, to see what we need to do in order to go about this.

> Proverbs 4:25 NIV: Let your eyes look straight ahead; fix your gaze directly before you.[88]

The Snapchat memory that popped up that day that shook me to my core and prompted me to write this chapter was a selfie of me where you could see just from my eyes up, and I had a blanket on top of my head. In the selfie I wrote to my friend about how badly my head was hurting in this moment and how I had no clue about what was going on that was causing me so much stress and anxiety. I remember waking up in the morning, checking my phone, and seeing how different my life was only a short amount of time ago.

I remember my wheels starting to turn and how I was anxious about the new life changes that were coming up at that point of my life, and how I had no idea of what to expect as I started a new journey of my life: college.

---

88 Bible Gateway. (2019). Bible Gateway Passage: Proverbs 4:25 – New International Version [online]

Looking back on that Snap really made me kind of sad to see how things were, but it also made me remember that my Savior pulled me straight out of those dark times that truly engulfed me at one point. Seeing those images and memories of how different things were just really blows my mind.

Looking at memories can be both good and bad. In this scenario, it was a good thing because I was able to thank the Lord for the millionth time for what He had done and continues to do in my life. It was also a good thing because I was able to find that reminder deep down inside of me that I made it, and that I won a battle that threatened and partially ran my life for a few months. It feels so good to be free now, but it is also really inspiring to look back on my past. The past is the past, but like it says in Proverbs 4:25, "Let your eyes look directly forward, and your gaze be straight before you." Don't let your past hinder you, and don't let it stir the pot too strongly emotionally, too much to the point where you crash and burn.

Also, remember that your past got you to where you are today. The Lord loves you no matter what you did, what happened to you, what you thought, or what you felt like in the past. He loves you and He knows you. He knows you by name, and He wants you to come to Him for safety and protection. The Lord is good and He wants to see you and know you. It is sometimes hard to look back on memories from past months or years, and that's okay. Accept that you feel that way and move forward. Don't let the bad memories keep you from pursuing things, and remember the good memories with a grateful heart. No matter where in life you are in this moment, always remember that these memories and your past have built you to be who you are today, and that's a pretty cool thing.

You now have this incredible story and testimony to share with others. You can show others your Snapchat memories if they are going through something you once went through. Always remember that the Lord does not put you through these hard times with hard memories for nothing. He does this so you can really dig deep and find the Light within yourself, and also so you can inspire someone else later on down the road. You will one day meet someone who is going through something very similar to you, or something similar to what you once went through. While the past is sometimes hard to accept, attempt to accept it for what it is and move forward. Use your experiences to build yourself stronger and to show other people it is okay to still be healing from it, or to show other people that it is okay to look back on those memories in a very nostalgic way.

Always remember that while times do come and go, there is always more room for more and more Snapchat memories. You will continue to make more memories, and if you feel like you are at a standstill right now in your life in terms of memories, think again, because something beautiful will happen soon. It always does, even if it's just something as simple as the Lord's artwork in the sky, or a butterfly that brushes right past you. Find the good in everything, snap a few pictures, put them in storage, and look at them later on. You will be thankful you did, because you never know what an answer to your prayer could look like.

END OF CHAPTER TAKEAWAYS:

BIBLE VERSES:
- Proverbs 4:25 ESV

QUESTIONS FOR TAKEAWAY:
- How do you use memories to enable you to grow?
- How can you also use memories for good, even if some of them are negative?

ACTIONABLE TAKEAWAYS:
- Reflect on your memories, even the ones that are less than desirable.
- Write down your memories, take pictures, and keep memorabilia. Do what you can to remember these times, both because it is important to remember and will also be powerful to look back on one day in the future.
- Hang up photos around your room and use them as reminders that even though you could be in a tough time, you will grow from it.

PRAYER:
Hey God. I am thankful for all of the memories, both the good and bad. While some days I will find something that brings back the negative, I trust and know that You will use it for good. I know who You are, and I know that You are good. I am thankful for all of the memories I have created and experienced, thanks to You. You have done so much in my life, and I am grateful. Amen.

CHAPTER 28

WITH YOU

———

Even when it feels as though everything is against you, and the waves are rough and the wind is quick, or when it feels that everyone is against you, just remember that the Lord is always with you. He who never fails, He who always comes and rescues us from our storms is always here.

The Lord is always with us, but it's also important for us to desire that close-knit relationship with Him. Once we grow in our faith, we will find the true understanding and fulfillment that comes from having that relationship with Him. The Lord desires that true relationship with you. He desires to see you seek Him in the midst of your busy days and in the midst of your quiet times. He desires to see you seek Him when you are crying and shaking because of fear, and He desires to see you seek Him when you are jumping for joy because your lifelong dream just became a reality.

The song "With You" by Elevation Worship is weighing heavily on my heart in this chapter, in a positive way. This song brings so much joy into my heart, by God's grace. It also makes me really pause and think about how amazing it is to be able to seek a Father who is in not only our hearts, but also our minds. He fulfills and fills every void and broken arrow in our minds.

The first time I heard this song, the declaration of having an anxious imagination and the statement that anxiety is just superficial stuck out like a sharp thorn on a bush, because it's true: anxiety is on the surface. Anxiety fills our minds and hearts with very tough ideas, but at the end of the day we know that there is a stronger vine that connects us to the peace that we desire. We also know that anxiety cannot destroy us. It may try to creep into our brain and our heart, but it cannot completely take over. The Lord will pull us from those situations and fill the voids and cracks with that perfect peace, but it is still incredibly essential to build and desire that strong relationship with Him.

When the lead singer of this song, Tiffany Hammer, sings to God about how solely being in His presence is her desired place, that hit home. At the end of the day, think about how amazing that perfect peace is with Him and how truly powerful it is that we can come home to Him. Saying that there is nowhere else I'd rather be is a very powerful yet humbling statement. It allows us to focus on the fact that our King is the One we need to fix our minds upon, and that we need to let go of everything else that comes to mind and embrace the fullness of His presence.

John 10:27 NIV: My sheep listen to my voice; I know them, and they follow me.[89]

One of my favorite parts in this song is when it talks about how it feels when you come into God's presence and you feel that calmness come over you, and you feel it fill every single void, crack, doubt, and imperfection. This magnifies how God pours into our brokenness. He uses our suffering for good and He will always find us, even in the darkest of nights.

The first time I ever heard this song was on a Sunday morning during my freshman year when I was watching an Elevation Church service online. When I heard the first lines of it, I knew there was a true reason why the Lord had me seated in that chair that morning listening with my full attention. I was dealing with a good bit of pressure and anxiety during this time of the year because of school and my classes, so to hear these words sung so calmly brought me to tears. I knew that the Lord was telling me then to be still and to come to Him. I knew He was telling me that everything would be okay and that I would get out of these hard times. Finally, I also knew that He was telling me to come home to Him—to stop worrying about everything and to just come home to Him, because He is the one who can give me peace and comfort no matter what the season or time is.

From that moment on, I knew that the Lord was about to show me how special and important it is to have a relationship

---

89 Bible Gateway. (2019). Bible Gateway Passage: John 10:27 – New International Version [online]

with Him—a good and strong one. I knew that the Lord was about to show up and work in my life and heal me from that anxiety. He did, and He did big time. Ever since that day, whenever I am anxious or stressed, I will turn that song on, lie down, and close my eyes, and just focus as much as I can on those words.

It is truly important to desire a strong relationship with Him, and to know that He can work in your life in unthinkable ways. It is important for us to remember that our relationship with Him is the most important relationship we could possibly have. He is the giver, the Light, and the Truth. He is everything, and above all things He is our Heavenly Father. He is the one who gives us peace; He desires to be with us so much, and He desires for us to want to be with Him as well.

2 Chronicles 15:2 NIV: The Lord is with you when you are with him. If you seek him, he will be found by you, but if you forsake him, he will forsake you.[90]

It's really impactful to think about how I listen to this song and move into a time of reflection and prayer with the Lord. My friend, Andrew Boyles, shared with me how it also brings him so much peace to offer something up to Him when he knows he can't do anything more for a given situation.

---

90 Bible Gateway. (2019). Bible Gateway Passage: 2 Chronicles 15:2 – New International Version [online]

Andrew made this great point:

"There is a universal truth in this world: there are always things that we cannot control, and that's alright, because it shows us that we aren't God. Now, I'm all for trying your best in every situation; in fact, I encourage it. But the fact remains that oftentimes there are a multitude of things that are out of your control in any given situation."

It's imperative to give these situations up and spend time with God and in His presence as He heals us from the hard times and trials. It's important for us to let God work, and to know that He is God and we are not.

We can't fix everything, and that is fine. We aren't called to bear the weight of our burdens as Christians; we are called to release our burdens to Him and to spend time in His perfect peace.

He loves us for who we are, and He simply wants us to spend time with Him. He is a God that provides perfect peace and who protects His people. He loves us and He made us in His perfect image, and He wants us to be free from fear and free from any shame we may wrestle with. He will always pull us from the hard times, and He will lead us through it all. As long as we seek Him, He will be right there with us. He will deliver us, and He will shine through the imagination that sometimes stirs our hearts in the worst ways.

Finally, Andrew makes this incredible point: "In this life and after death, you know that God is there, and that He loves you, and because of this love, you will be saved." When you are with Him, you are saved. You will find His goodness and His glory, and you will learn what His grace feels like and is.

We love to spend time with Him, but He loves spending time with us. This love He has for us is so great and it truly will be a huge part of that perfect peace we desire. Like my Uncle Harold says, as long as we trust in Him, the Holy Spirit will do great works in our lives. We need to trust in Him and trust this process.

He will never leave us. Always remember that the negative thoughts firing throughout your head are your imagination. The Devil is sending them to throw you off your path and to shake you up. The Lord only sends positive ones, and He will fill those cracks like always.

END OF CHAPTER TAKEAWAYS:

BIBLE VERSES:
- John 10:27 NIV
- 2 Chronicles 15:2 NIV

QUESTIONS FOR REFLECTION:
- How do you feel when you are with your friends and family?
- Think about how it feels when you are with God—meaning, in His presence—and you are spending time with Him. How does that make you feel?
- How will you seek Him and spend time with Him, even in the busiest of seasons?

- Manage time with God and remember to do it daily.
- Listen to the song "With You" by Elevation Worship.
- Take time to dive in and to seek Him and His goodness wherever you are.

PRAYER:

Heavenly Father, I am truly in awe of You. I am so thankful of Your goodness, and I am so thankful and empowered by how incredible it is when I am in Your presence. I thank You for Your endless grace, and for all things that You do. I know that You supply me with Your riches, and I thank You for that. I know that You are good, and I pray that You will allow me to see that for all of my days, even the days in which I feel far from You. Amen.

CHAPTER 29

OVERWHELMED

———

As I write this, I am currently sitting here feeling all of these emotions. I am sitting on my comfy bed right by the window in my newly decorated apartment, preparing to dive into my sophomore year at Clemson University. My mind was racing with thoughts of, "How on earth am I going to finish this book?" and "How am I going to write Bible studies for my sorority?" Then I decided to take some time for just Jesus and me. Boy, was that revolutionary, just like always. While listening to the song "Be Still" by Hillsong United, my mind flipped like a switch and I remembered some important things:

- *I have genuinely made it through every single hard thing that has come my way, and I know I will have the strength and will to continue to move forward through the hard things that come my way, by the grace of God.*

And, friend, so can you. He will lead you through all of the disasters and hardships that come your way. No mess can amount to what God has in store for you, and He will lead you through the shattered and broken pieces.

- *The people who have caused any pain and harm have all given me knowledge that will enable me to move forward in life and to know how to handle tough situations.*

It's very easy for us to just shun people who have hurt our hearts and minds, and while we need to remove toxic people from our lives, it is essential that we continue to pray for them. Be the bigger person, step up to the plate, and swing for the fence. Pray for them and hope that He will heal their heart as well as yours. Sometimes the people who have caused pain in our lives actually provide great wisdom. We learn about things that we want in life (such as what we look for in a potential significant other) or things we don't want to be a part of our lives.

- *Anxiety, once again, does not have a hold on my life anymore. It cannot and will not win. The Mighty Lion roars inside of me and defeats the tiny gnat of anxiety that tries to break Him down.*

Your struggle, whatever that may look like, does not have a hold on your life. It is no match for God. God is mightier and far more powerful than whatever your struggle may look like. He will deliver you from your struggles, and He will provide so much for your heart and mind. Trust Him, and know that He is the ultimate redeemer.

Anxiety is a situation that—while difficult—is something that can be beat. The Lord will always give you the strength and drive to persevere, move through the hard times, and continue to grow as you go. Anxiety is one of those things that is thought to be unbreakable, but in reality, God is the unbreakable One! He is the One who can change your life and pull you through the broken and hard times. He's a God who will never leave you when you have a moment where you slip.

John 15:11 NIV: I have told you this so that my joy may be in you and that your joy may be complete.[91]

I am overwhelmed. I am overwhelmed by how God has shown up in my life despite me being in complete ruin at times. I am overwhelmed by the love and support my friends and family give me and have given me in the past. I am overwhelmed by the positivity and encouragement I receive from New Degree Press, the company that is publishing this book and helping me make my little girl dream turn into a big girl reality. I am overwhelmed by God's grace. I am overwhelmed by the love and kindness coming from all around me.

I am overwhelmed in the best way. Not in an anxiety-ridden state. Not in a fearful or shaking manner. I am overwhelmed. Simply overwhelmed, and I am thankful.

Every single message. Every single prayer. Every single smile. Every single tear. All of it has brought me here to this point of healing. I am still healing from some of the things I have

---

91   Bible Gateway. (2019). Bible Gateway Passage: John 15:11 – New International Version [online]

dealt with in the past, but I have been privileged enough to witness my own personal growth during these times.

Always remember that all of the hard times will blossom and turn, just like the leaves change in the fall into something beautiful. You could be sitting on your couch with a pile of things to do around you, and a whole other list of things to do on your laptop. You could be in the midst of one of the hardest seasons of your life preparing for your dream. Wherever you are right now, in this moment, just stop. Look at the ceiling, the sky ... just up. Look up, and remind yourself that despite your present situation, you will find the goodness you so desire. You will soon feel overwhelmed in the best possible way like I do right now.

On your hardest days, on that day when you receive soul-crushing news, you're exhausted from a breakup, or you're just flat out not in the mood, look back and remember that you have survived every single one of your hardest days. You may look back and remember some days you barely thought you would get through, but hold true in your heart and mind that you did it. You made it through them all and God is going to bring you right through all of the rest of the hard days that happen.

You may think you are too far gone, or too far away from God to find His grace and to learn more about Him. You may feel unworthy to learn about Him or to feel Him. You may feel like you are unworthy of His grace and unworthy of His vision for your life. You are worthy. You deserve this. You deserve to receive His grace and His abundant love for you, and to feel Him all around you. You deserve to be able to look at yourself in the mirror in the morning and to see yourself how God sees you: beautiful and amazing in every way and created in His perfect image. You deserve to feel overwhelmed by God's grace when you fall on your knees during worship because of how His word and the song have impacted you and shot like an arrow through your heart. You deserve that, and He knows that. That is why He sent His one and only Son to die for us and for our sins ... to save us all.

Philippians 4:13 NIV: I can do all this through him who gives me strength.[92]

I am overwhelmed when I realize that while I still suffer from some of the physical parts of anxiety, I can say I have defeated anxiety by God's grace, many times. I won my life back. Again and again, as the waves roll in and cause the ship to buckle, I still win my life back. That's all because of Jesus and His mercy and His undying love for us. Having an anxiety disorder is never easy, but having God's grace always filling my heart makes it that much easier.

Now, I must clarify here: when I say that by God's grace I have defeated anxiety many times, what I mean is that I still deal with my anxiety disorder since it IS an actual disorder. I just know where to turn and Who to call on, and Who to always focus my heart and mind on. It makes things a little

---

92 Bible Gateway. (2019). Bible Gateway Passage: Philippians 4:13 – New International Version [online]

easier, even when my heart is beating fast and my palms are a bit sweaty.

Even when you are overwhelmed, your heart feels heavy, and you are dragging yourself around mentally or physically, know that you CAN do it. As Philippians 4:13 says, I can do all things through Christ who strengthens me. He will give you the strength to follow Him and to run back to His open arms even when everything is against you. When your own mind and heart are rumbling with fear, or just sullen with sadness, He will give you strength to pull yourself back up, and He will be right next to you pulling you up. He will give you strength to find the ability to pursue your dreams … those dreams you thought would never happen. The things that just seem impossible aren't so impossible when you have Jesus in your heart. Allow Him to pull the weight and trust in Him, spread His name and Word, and pray. Stay truthful to yourself and to Him, and He will do incredible things in your life.

Anxiety and depression are no match for God. PTSD is no match for God. Eating disorders are no match for God. Trauma is no match for God. Suicidal thoughts are no match for God. There is NO MATCH for our Heavenly Father! Let Him in. Let Him free your heart and soul. Let Him yank the Devil's filthy hands away from your heart and mind, and provide peace for your heart and mind. The Father wants our minds to be a safe and comfortable place, not a place of torment and constant turmoil. Turn your heart and mind to God let your heart be restless for His goodness, and let your mind be hopeful in anticipation for what He can do next.

Psalm 4:8 NIV: In peace I will lie down
and sleep,
for you alone, Lord,
make me dwell in safety.[93]

Every single leg of this journey has given you the ability to learn much more about yourself and about how you handle things. No matter how many times you hassle with it, no matter how many times you have to defeat it, it will continue to strengthen you and allow you to build your heart from Christ. A movie I watched for a course on religion at Clemson, *God on Trial*, said this quote: "A great fire only grows greater." I don't remember the context from which that was said, but what stuck out to me is how once you have that fire burning in your heart, it will continue to grow. Add fuel to your fire. Read the Word, worship, and stay in community. Build your life, and ignite that fire; continue building, brick by brick. God will do the heavy lifting and keep the wood burning; you need only be still.

END OF CHAPTER TAKEAWAYS:

BIBLE VERSES:

- John 15:11 NIV
- Philippians 4:13 NIV
- Psalms 4:8 NIV

---

93 Bible Gateway. (2019). Bible Gateway Passage: Psalm 4:8 – New International Version [online]

QUESTIONS FOR REFLECTION:

- When you are overwhelmed, is this feeling normally positive or negative?
- How do you manage these feelings, given the situation (positive versus negative emotions)?
- How do you think God can use you even when you are feeling overwhelmed about things?
- How have you seen God work even when you are overwhelmed?

ACTIONABLE TAKEAWAYS:

- Practice square breathing as mentioned earlier in this book as a means to calm down. This is an essential tactic for whenever you are in a stressful or high-energy state that is leading you to be overwhelmed.
- Breathe in for four, breathe out for four, and do this four times.
- On a sticky note or on something you see a lot (such as a desktop wallpaper, phone background, or agenda) write "_____ is no match for God."
  - In the blank, put whatever you are struggling with or dealing with in that moment, and keep it handy.
- Stay consistent in prayer so that it becomes your first-choice defense.

PRAYER:

Heavenly Father, I am in awe of all You are doing in my life. While it can be a little scary, and a little nerve-wracking, I know that You are good through it all. I have seen You transform millions of lives around me in the most amazing ways, and I can't wait to see how You work in my life. I am overwhelmed, and I am praying for calmness and to focus on You, and the ability to recognize the next steps. Amen.

CHAPTER 30

IT IS WELL

———

Mark 5:34 NIV: He said to her, "Daughter, your faith has healed you. Go in peace and be freed from your suffering."[94]

By God's grace, I can now say I have defeated anxiety.

Day by day, hour by hour, I am being healed from the disease that has robbed my peace and tranquility for too long now. I am being healed from the scars that ravaged through my heart, that tore me down. That made me feel guilty for the anxiety I deal with, even though it is truly biological.

My faith has made me well. I am safe, I am happy, and I am healed. All in His name.

———

94 Bible Gateway. (2019). Bible Gateway Passage: Mark 5:34 – New International Version [online]

Writing these words, finally and truthfully, is such a powerful statement to me.

The key to this statement is the knowledge that I am NOT bound by my anxiety, the Devil's lies, and the untruth that surrounds them. I may still deal with anxiety from time to time, after all, and so will you, because we are human. However, being able to say you defeated it means that you have defeated the large amount of discomfort that comes with these feelings. You have defeated the ultimate hold and chains that you were once bound by. You now are more in control, by God's grace, to solve these problems and to give the Lord the means to jump in and pull you from the fire.

You have defeated the demons inside of your heart. You are not bound by this pain; you are free. You are experiencing this freedom as we speak, and the Devil no longer has such a hold anymore. Being able to speak and declare that your struggle doesn't have any hold over you is such a powerful accomplishment and moment. It shouldn't be taken lightly, and it should always be trusted. God will do so many incredible things.

John 11:40 NIV: Then Jesus said, "Did I not tell you that if you believe, you will see the glory of God?"[95]

95 Bible Gateway. (2019). Bible Gateway Passage: John 11:40 – New International Version [online]

Over time, I have heard from so many people who have dealt with the same thing as I have, regarding faith and mental health—for example, from Pastor Steven, Holly Furtick, and my own ministers back at home, and the Lord speaking through unconventional means to help me with my anxiety. I have seen Instagram posts and tweets that have provided so much encouragement and motivation to continue to fight my way through the forests. I have met so many incredible people over just the past year of my life who have encouraged me and prayed for me during this fight. It is so important to find people and things that will help you grow through this storm, because it really will help enable you to grow and to chase your dreams, without feeling the weight of your burdens.

You will see His glory. You will see it when your chains are lifted day by day, you will see it as your heart calms from the staggering anxiety racing through. You will see it when you are able to pull yourself out of bed and do the tasks you need to get done. You will see His glory no matter where you are. You will see His glory for your drive to know Him and His heart. His glory will wash over you like the waves wash over the sand on a beach.

John 16:33 NIV: "I have told you these things, so that in me you may have peace. In this world you will have trouble. But take heart! I have overcome the world."[96]

---

96 Bible Gateway. (2019). Bible Gateway Passage: John 16:33 – New International Version [online]

At the end of the day, anxiety and these mental health disorders we suffer from will not win. They do not have a hold on us anymore. The Lord has saved us from not only the Devil, but also ourselves, and for that, I am thankful. Extremely thankful. God has overcome the world, and we need to be thankful. We need to be thankful that we are truly released from the shackles and chains by which we were once bound. He has risen, and He has overcome.

Do not let it win. Do not let the Devil win and tear you away from Christ. The Devil plays games, but the Lord always wins them.

It seems challenging and it seems hard, because when you think about my story you may be wondering how a girl who has a clinically diagnosed mental health disorder can defeat it—not just once, but multiple times—and my answer to you is 100 percent, hands down God. I would not be who I am today if it weren't for how the Lord has consistently swooped in and saved me from the flames that threaten to engulf me. I wouldn't be who I am today if it weren't for the hard times and suffering I had gone through to strengthen and enable me. Finally, I also wouldn't be who I am today if I didn't have the support system I have.

One of the most important concepts and principles to understand to ultimately defeat your struggle is that you need to surround yourself with positive influences. Like Maci Bolin shared, you need to surround yourself with individuals who will always love you for you and who see the good in you. You need to surround yourself with people who will tell you the truth even if it hurts sometimes, because these words will ultimately strengthen you. You need to surround yourself with Christian figures who know exactly what you're going through in your periods of doubt.

As you have read throughout this book, the Lord works in mysterious and big ways. Earlier this week, I prayed to the Lord, "How much longer, Lord?" I meant how much longer will this anxiety last, when I knew that He was delivering me from it. I prayed this prayer because the day-to-day anxiety was largely gone, but the anxiety was now in my dreams. I remember hearing the Lord boldly and loudly saying, "You're almost there." Five days later, I went to church and the worship band sang the songs "Done," "Forever I Run," "Better Word," and "With You," all by Elevation Worship. In that moment, I felt something big shift. The stone that had been cast on my heart and brain for quite some time was finally dissolving, by the grace of God.

I can't sit here and write to you and tell you I will never have an anxious thought again. That, quite frankly, is impossible. But what is possible, however, is that the Lord has and will continue to deliver me from these thoughts as they arise. I now have the tools and mechanisms to find peace even in the hardest times of struggle. You too shall have this peace once you give it to Christ. He will give you the ability, tools, and resources to manage your struggle, even if it is just during times of stress. No story is too little, and no story deserves to be looked down on. Always remember that you matter, and the Lord wants you to come to Him with your problems because His opinion of you will never change. He created you in His perfect image, and He loves you exactly the way you are.

Your struggle does not, and never will, define you. You may have chosen to read this book because you were newly diagnosed with a mental health struggle or some other struggle you have been dealing with for a while. You may have chosen to read this book just because you thought the cover looked pretty or intriguing. You may have chosen to read this book because you know me or know someone who recommended this book. Regardless of why and how you came across this book, and no matter what you deal with in your life, this same victory can happen for you, as long as you give the distraction and the issue to the Lord entirely.

He wants all of you and all of your struggles, not just pieces and broken shards of it. In "With You" by Elevation Worship, they sing about wanting to know Him in His entirety, and how He desires for us to have that want. This shows how the Lord wants us in our entirety, not just the little pieces, and how we should desire to be close to Christ in that same manner; to truly know Him. Give all of your glory, pain, hurt, happiness, and everything else to the Lord. He will give you abundant grace, love, and peace.

The Lord will always save you from the storm you are in. The storm will not win; you and the Lord will. You may be stranded on that ship in the middle of the ocean, but never forget who will ultimately come back to rescue you in an unimaginable yet believable way. Your lifeguard. Your Savior.

It is Well.

AUTHOR'S NOTE

And now, we rest. We can rest in the fullness and truth of the Lord's great promises and desires for our lives. We can rest in the knowledge of true and everlasting safety that we have thanks to the Lord. We can rest in the truth that these mental health disorders and other struggles do not have a hold on our lives, and that that weight has been lifted. We can rest in the reality that we have been freed from the chains that bound our hearts and minds from the peace the Lord so readily desires to provide.

Through writing this book, I have really found my passion for writing, even more so than what I had before. Writing is a way that my soul can unleash the thunder that rumbles, the cheers that roar, and the fear that provokes. Writing is my outlet for the stressful times, and I pray that you will find an outlet or pour your energy into something you already have. However, as you may know, this book was somewhat tough for me to write. I had to fight a lot of doubt in order to complete this book. While writing this book, I was definitely dealing with some very confusing obstacles that were running right alongside of the book, meaning at the exact same time I was writing it. Those obstacles, as mentioned throughout the book, strengthened and enabled me overall, but in the moment caused a lot of laziness in regard to the completion of this book.

Despite dealing with a number of weird and odd circumstances, with anxiety as the undesired extra, I can say that I have healed and my heart is healing from the experiences I have endured, and that is forever a blessing.

I also want to say that I am proud of you. I am proud of you for reading this book, because I know mental health is a very triggering and emotional topic that is still viewed as somewhat taboo. I am proud of you for how far you have come throughout your life. I am proud that you are reading this book, because this is a way you are allowing yourself to move forward to bigger things and to break the chains. I am proud of you for continuing with your desires, and for continuing to work hard. I pray that you will never give up on anything you desire to do. This life is full of crazy things that seem impossible, but with the Lord and a lot of faith, you can do anything you set your mind to.

I would like to give a very special thank you to my family, my friends, and everyone I have met along the way of this journey—not just this book-writing journey, but throughout my life. I thank you for the support you have given me, and I am so thankful that you have given me the energy and drive to write and complete this book. Thank you.

Thank you once again for reading this book. This book holds a very near and dear place in my heart. With this book, I feel that you just read a chapter of my life. A chapter of my life is largely in words, and that is both terrifying yet amazing to me. With the ending of this book, I believe that you are reading and witnessing a chapter of my life closing and a new door opening.

God bless you, and thank you.

ROSE MARIE NEWSOM
"GG, Tootsie, Momma, Friend"

November 21, 1919—April 12, 2018

I hope we're making you proud...
We miss you and love you so much.

PHOTO SECTION

ACKNOWLEDGMENTS

——

First and foremost, I would like to thank my family for supporting me. It is incredible to have such a loving and supportive family who motivates me and wants to see my growth. To my parents, I am beyond thankful for y'all. Thank you for always motivating me and for supporting me in all of my dreams: the dream to attend Clemson University, the dream to be a teacher, the dream to help others, and the dream to publish this book. Thank you for your unrelenting support and care. To my sister Elizabeth, I am so thankful for you. Thank you for randomly FaceTiming me just for us to laugh and goof off for a good while, and thanks for being you. To my grandparents, Grammy and Bop Bop, I am so thankful for y'all as well. Thank you for supporting me no matter what and for always being there. I am thankful for y'all and I am thankful to have y'all in my life as mentors. To the rest of my family, I am so thankful for y'all as well and I thank y'all for your support, prayers, and love.

To my incredible college, Clemson University. Thank you for motivating me and for shaping me into the person I am today. I am so thankful for all of my professors, fellow Tigers, and friends. Thank you to Sigma Alpha Omega (Alpha Omicron chapter) for your prayers, love, positivity, and support during this process, and thank you to Clemson FCA for being such an incredible organization that has wrecked my heart time and time again → thanks to both Clemson University and Clemson FCA for molding me into who I am today.

Thank you to fellow Clemson Tiger, Marilyn Hazlett, for leading me to this opportunity to publish this book through Clemson Creators. Thank you to Professor Eric Koester from Georgetown University for starting the Creator Institute as a means for college students to publish books, and for spreading this to colleges all around.

Thank you to my hometown of Greenville, South Cariolina. Thank you to my former schools for the support and love during this process, and for encouraging me to be who I am today. Thank you to Dancers Corner for being a place where I sort of grew up. Thank you for loving and supporting me no matter what, no matter my abilities. Thank you to Mauldin United Methodist Church for being such an encouraging church family and for all of the support throughout this process.

Thank you to those who allowed me to interview them, and thanks to those who preordered. All of you played a huge role in this journey, and I am in awe of how it came to life, thanks to you.

Lastly, a HUGE thank you to the New Degree Press, especially Eric Koester, Brian Bies, and Linda Beradelli, for all of the support and motivation during this time ... and for getting my work published! Thank you for opening your minds and arms to my work and for caring for it so tenderly.

SPECIAL THANKS TO ALL WHO SUPPORTED:

Alex Ainspan

Allison McDonald

Amelia Sizemore

Amy and Jess Fortune

Anastasia Ehlers

Andrew Boyles

Anjali Patnam

Dr. Ann Bynum

Anjali Patnam

Amelia Sizemore

Amy and Jess Fortune

Bailee Hayden

Bailey Gotthiner

Bailey McMahon

Bess Skenteris

Beverly and Mark Lemmons

Billie Tuvshinbayar

Boykin Family

Bren Fousek

Carmen Burgess

Caroline Case

Carolyn Ledbetter

Carpenter Family

Carrie Ropp

Cathy Fousek

Cathy Morgan

Celeste Marchant

Christina Custodio

Ashley Cramton and family

Danielle Edwards

David and Heather Green

Debbie Edwards

Debbie McCroy

Dora Evans

Elaine and Larry Fousek

Elizabeth Newman

Eric Koester

Dr. Gary Jackson

Grace Ehlers

Grace Werner

Gracyn Taylor

Griffin Germond

Haleigh Dyson

Hannah Hildreth

Harold King

Hunter Johnson

Ian Leigh

Jack Lenhardt

Jamie Garland

Jason Blackwell

Jennifer Murphy

Kailey McCleod

Kelly, Mike, and Elizabeth Radecki

Kelsey Drzewicki
Kristina Sisk
Kylee Trangmar
Laura Nelson
Lauren Hogan
Lisa Fagan
Lisa Fowler
Liz Hammar
Lori Farmer
Lucianne Cassles
Lynn Deese Wood
Mallory Ware
Marilyn Hazlett
Mary Heaton
Mary Ropp
Melissa Hudson

Michelle Ashley
Michelle McKee & family
Mike Peake
Mollie Warren
Monica Radecki
Palmer Fousek
Pamela Stroot
Patrick Goodwin
Paws Diner
Rebecca Lesley
Rich Gooding
Samantha Decker
Sandra Teague
Stacy Durrell
Taft Matney
Turner Prewitt

One final thanks as well goes to the church community that supported my project so graciously. I am in awe of you, and if you are reading this, then you know who you are. Thank you.

CITATIONS

———

INTRODUCTION:

Quinn, N., Wilson, A., MacIntyre, G. and Tinklin, T. (2009). *'People look at you differently': students' experience of mental health support within Higher Education.* [online] Taylor & Francis. Available at: https://www.tandfonline.com/doi/full/10.1080/03069880903161385

CHAPTER 1, THE SHIP:

Bible Gateway. (2019). *Bible Gateway Passage: Jeremiah 29:11 – New International Version* [online] Available at: https://www.biblegateway.com/passage/?search=Jeremiah+29%3A11+&version=NIV

CHAPTER 2, FEAR IS A LIAR:

Bible Gateway. (2019). *Bible Gateway Passage: Isaiah 41:10 – New International Version* [online] Available at: https://www.biblegateway.com/passage/?search=Isaiah+41%3A10+&version=NIV

Bible Gateway. (2019). *Bible Gateway Passage: 1 Peter 5:10 – New International Version* [online] Available at: https://www. biblegateway.com/passage/?search=1+Peter+5&version=ESV

Flip It | Flip the Flow | Pastor Steven Furtick. (2019). [video] Directed by S. Furtick. Elevation Church: Elevation Church.

CHAPTER 3, EVEN IF:

Bible Gateway. (2019). *Bible Gateway Passage: Daniel 3:17 – New International Version*. [online] Available at: https://www.biblegateway.com/ passage/?search=Daniel+3%3A17&version=NIV

Bible Gateway. (2019). *Bible Gateway Passage: Job 3:20-23 – New International Version*. [online] Available at: https:// www.biblegateway.com/passage/?search=Job+3:20-23&version=NIV

Bible Gateway. (2019) *Bible Gateway Passage: Job 42:12 New International Version* [online] Available at: https://www. biblegateway.com/passage/?search=job+42:12&version=NIV

Bible Gateway. (2019) *Bible Gateway Passage: John 11:35 New International Version* [online] Available at: https://www. biblegateway.com/passage/?search=John+11:35&version=NIV

Law, J. (2019). *MercyMe's Frontman Bart Millard Pens 'Even If' Song on Heartbreak Over Son's Chronic Illness*. [online] Christianpost.com. Available at: https://www.christianpost. com/news/mercymes-frontman-bart-millard-pens-even-if-song-on-heartbreak-over-sons-chronic-illness.html

CHAPTER 4, WON'T STOP NOW:

Bible Gateway. (2019). *Bible Gateway Passage: Deuteronomy 31:8 – New International Version.* [online] Available at: https://www.biblegateway.com/passage/?search=Deuteronomy+31%3A8&version=NIV

Bible Gateway. (2019). *Bible Gateway Passage: Deuteronomy 31:6 – New International Version.* [online] Available at: https://www.biblegateway.com/passage/?search=Deuteronomy+31%3A6&version=NIV

Bible Gateway. (2019). *Bible Gateway Passage: Psalm 147:3 – New International Version.* [online] Available at: https://www.biblegateway.com/passage/?search=psalm+147%3A3&version=NIV

CHAPTER 5, WHY AM I ANXIOUS?

"5 Surprising Mental Health Statistics." 2019. Mental Health First Aid. February 6, 2019. https://www.mentalhealthfirstaid.org/2019/02/5-surprising-mental-health-statistics/

Bible Gateway. (2019). *Bible Gateway Passage: Psalm 139:23 – New International Version.* [online] Available at: https://www.biblegateway.com/passage/?search=psalm+139%3A23&version=NIV

Bible Gateway. (2019). *Bible Gateway Passage: Psalm 139:24 – New International Version.* [online] Available at: https://www.biblegateway.com/passage/?search=psalm+139%3A24&version=NIV

Bible Gateway. (2019). *Bible Gateway Passage: Isaiah 41:10 – New International Version* [online] Available at: https://www.biblegateway.com/ passage/?search=Isaiah+41%3A10+&version=NIV

Goldberg, Joseph. "Mental Health: The Brain and Mental Illness." WebMD, WebMD, April 6, 2019. https://www. webmd.com/mental-health/brain-mental-illness

Elevation Church. *"Why Am I Anxious? | Bars & Battles | Pastor Steven Furtick"* Youtube video, posted August 2017.

CHAPTER 6, THE HOPE CYCLE:

Bible Gateway. (2019). *Bible Gateway Passage: 1 Peter 5:10 – New International Version* [online] Available at: https://www. biblegateway.com/passage/?search=1+Peter+5&version=ESV

Bible Gateway. (2019). *Bible Gateway Passage: Romans 5:3-4 – New International Version [online]* Available at: https:// www.biblegateway.com/passage/?search=romans+5%3A+3- 4&version=NIV

Elevation Church. *"The Hope Cycle | Holly Furtick"* Youtube video, posted May 2019. https://youtu.be/gJ3JSATgCOI

CHAPTER 7, THE TRENCH

Bible Gateway. (2019). *Bible Gateway Passage: Matthew 11:28 – New International Version* [online] Available at: https://www.biblegateway.com/ passage/?search=matthew+11%3A28+&version=NIV

CHAPTER 8, THE GOOD FIGHT

Bible Gateway. (2019). *Bible Gateway Passage: 2 Timothy 4:7-8 – New International Version* [online] Available at: https://www.biblegateway.com/passage/?search=2+Timothy+4%3A+7-8+&version=NIV

Bible Gateway. (2019). *Bible Gateway Passage: Psalm 108:13 – New International Version* [online] Available at: https://www.biblegateway.com/passage/?search=psalm+108%3A13&version=NIV

Flip It | Flip the Flow | Pastor Steven Furtick. (2019). [video] Directed by S. Furtick. Elevation Church: Elevation Church.

CHAPTER 9, ALL IN, ALL THE TIME

Bible Gateway. (2019). *Bible Gateway Passage: James 1:2 – New International Version* [online] Available at: https://www.biblegateway.com/passage/?search=James+1%3A12&version=NIV

Bible Gateway. (2019). *Bible Gateway Passage: Galatians 6:9 – New International Version* [online] Available at: https://www.biblegateway.com/passage/?search=galatians+6%3A9&version=NIV

Bible Gateway. (2019). *Bible Gateway Passage: Proverbs 21:31 – New International Version* [online] Available at: https://www.biblegateway.com/passage/?search=proverbs+21%3A31&version=NIV

"Clemson Coach Dabo Swinney: Jesus Helps Me 'Survive and Thrive'." 2019. Sports Spectrum. October 29, 2019. https://sportsspectrum.com/sport/football/2018/07/20/clemsons-dabo-swinney-jesus-helps-me-survive-and-thrive/

Dabo Swinney, Clemson Football. (2017). Twitter. https://twitter.com/ClemsonFB/status/871873172097966080

CHAPTER 10, LOCATIONS

Bible Gateway. (2019). *Bible Gateway Passage: Psalm 4:8 – New International Version* [online] Available at: https://www.biblegateway.com/passage/?search=psalm+4%3A8+&version=NIV

CHAPTER 11, SURROUNDED

Bible Gateway. (2019). *Bible Gateway Passage: James 4:8 – New International Version* [online] Available at: https://www.biblegateway.com/passage/?search=James+4%3A8&version=NIV

Bible Gateway. (2019). *Bible Gateway Passage: 2 Corinthians 5:7 – New International Version* [online] Available at: https://www.biblegateway.com/passage/?search=2+corinthians+5%3A7+&version=NIV

"Mental Health in America." 2019. Bradley University Online. September 24, 2019. https://onlinedegrees.bradley.edu/blog/mental-health-in-america/

CHAPTER 12, FOLLOWING THE ROAD LESS TRAVELED

Bible Gateway. (2019). *Bible Gateway Passage: Jeremiah 29:11 – New International Version* [online] Available at: https://www.biblegateway.com/passage/?search=Jeremiah+29%3A11+&version=NIV

Bible Gateway. (2019). *Bible Gateway Passage: John 8:12 – New International Version* [online] Available at: https://www.biblegateway.com/passage/?search=John+8%3A12&version=NIV

Bible Gateway. (2019). *Bible Gateway Passage: Psalm 119:105 – New International Version* [online] Available at: https://www.biblegateway.com/passage/?search=psalm+119%3A105&version=NIV

CHAPTER 13, LAND OF THE FREE — BECAUSE OF THE BRAVE

Bible Gateway. (2019). *Bible Gateway Passage: John 15:13 – New International Version* [online] Available at: https://www.biblegateway.com/passage/?search=John+15%3A13&version=NIV

Bible Gateway. (2019). *Bible Gateway Passage: Isaiah 40:29 – New International Version* [online] Available at: https://www.biblegateway.com/passage/?search=Isaiah+40%3A29&version=NIV

Branch, John. 2008. "The Track That Defied the Writing on the Wall." The New York Times. The New York Times. May 10, 2008. https://www.nytimes.com/2008/05/10/

sports/othersports/10darlington.html?scp=1&sq=harold l
king&st=cse

Katie Moisee | ABC News. 2013. "Former Navy SEAL Chris
Kyle's Killing Puts Spotlight on PTSD". ABCNews.go.
February 3, 2013. Available at: https://abcnews.go.com/
Health/death-navy-seal-chris-kyle-puts-spotlight-ptsd/
story?id=18393163

Office of Suicide Prevention and Mental Health, United
States Department of Veteran Affairs, (2017). *Suicide
Among Veterans and Other Americans 2001–
2014*. Available at: https://www.mentalhealth.va.gov/
docs/2016suicidedatareport.pdf

Sarah Pulliam Bailey | Religion News Service. 2015. "Here's
the Faith in the 'American Sniper' You Won't See in the
Film." The Washington Post. WP Company. January 14, 2015.
Available at: https://www.washingtonpost.com/national/
religion/heres-the-faith-in-the-american-sniper-you-
wont-see-in-the-film/2015/01/14/f7c33bd6-9c0a-11e4-86a3-
1b56f64925f6_story.html

Schmidle, Nicholas. 2019. "In the Crosshairs." The New Yorker.
The New Yorker. July 10, 2019. https://www.newyorker.com/
magazine/2013/06/03/in-the-crosshairs.

CHAPTER 14, KING OF MY HEART

Bible Gateway. (2019). *Bible Gateway Passage:
Luke 6:28 – New International Version*

[online] Available at: https://www.biblegateway.com/
passage/?search=Luke+6%3A28+&version=NIV

Bible Gateway. (2019). *Bible Gateway Passage:
Philippians 4:19 – New International Version*
[online] Available at: https://www.biblegateway.com/
passage/?search=Philippians+4%3A19&version=NIV

CHAPTER 15, BEAUTIFUL CREATURES

Bible Gateway. (2019). *Bible Gateway Passage:
Genesis 1:27 – New International Version*
[online] Available at: https://www.biblegateway.com/
passage/?search=genesis+1%3A27&version=NIV

Bible Gateway. (2019). *Bible Gateway Passage:
Psalm 139:14 – New International Version*
[online] Available at: https://www.biblegateway.com/
passage/?search=psalm+139%3A14&version=NIV

CHAPTER 16, LAY YOUR BURDENS DOWN

Bible Gateway. (2019). *Bible Gateway Passage: Philippains 4:6-7 –
New International Version* [online] Available at: https://www.
biblegateway.com/passage/?search=Philippians+4%3A6-
7&version=NIV

Bible Gateway. (2019). *Bible Gateway Passage:
Matthew 11:28 – New International Version*
[online] Available at: https://www.biblegateway.com/
passage/?search=Matthew+11%3A28&version=NIV

CHAPTER 17, WHAT DOES FAITH MEAN TO YOU?

Bible Gateway. (2019). *Bible Gateway Passage: 2 Corinthians 5:7 – New International Version* [online] Available at: https://www.biblegateway.com/passage/?search=2+corinthians+5%3A7+&version=NIV

Bible Gateway. (2019). *Bible Gateway Passage: Ephesians 2:8 – New International Version* [online] Available at: https://www.biblegateway.com/passage/?search=Ephesians+2%3A8+&version=NIV

Bible Gateway. (2019). *Bible Gateway Passage: Isaiah 58:11 – New International Version* [online] Available at: https://www.biblegateway.com/passage/?search=Isaiah+58%3A11+&version=NIV

Bible Gateway. (2019). *Bible Gateway Passage: Matthew 17:20 – New International Version* [online] Available at: https://www.biblegateway.com/passage/?search=Matthew+17%3A20+&version=NIV

Bible Gateway. (2019). *Bible Gateway Passage: Matthew 21:21 – New International Version* [online] Available at: https://www.biblegateway.com/passage/?search=Matthew+21%3A21&version=NIV

CHAPTER 18, CHANGE

Bible Gateway. (2019). *Bible Gateway Passage: John 14:27 – New International Version* [online] Available at: https://www.biblegateway.com/passage/?search=John+14%3A27+&version=NIV

Bible Gateway. (2019). *Bible Gateway Passage: Matthew 6:34 – New International Version [online]* Available at: https://www.biblegateway.com/passage/?search=Matthew+6%3A34&version=NIV

Miller, Korin. 2017. "11 Little Mental Health Tips That Therapists Actually Give Their Patients." SELF. 2017. https://www.self.com/story/11-little-mental-health-tips-that-therapists-actually-give-their-patients.

CHAPTER 19, SIMPLE TRUTH

Bible Gateway. (2019). *Bible Gateway Passage: Isaiah 40:29 – New International Version [online]* Available at: https://www.biblegateway.com/passage/?search=Isaiah+40%3A29&version=NIV

Bible Gateway. (2019). *Bible Gateway Passage: 2 Corinthians 12:7-10 – New International Version [online]* Available at: https://www.biblegateway.com/passage/?search=2+corinthians+12%3A7-10&version=NIV

Clayton King. Stronger: How Hard Times Reveal God's Greatest Power. Page 50.

Clayton King. Stronger: How Hard Times Reveal God's Greatest Power. Page 50.

Clayton King. Stronger: How Hard Times Reveal God's Greatest Power. Page 51.

CHAPTER 20, SELF HELP

Bible Gateway. (2019). *Bible Gateway Passage: 2 Corinthians 3:17 – New International Version [online]* Available at: https://www.biblegateway.com/passage/?search=2+corinthians+3%3A17+&version=NIV

Bible Gateway. (2019). *Bible Gateway Passage: Exodus 14:14 – New International Version [online]* Available at: https://www.biblegateway.com/passage/?search=exodus+14%3A14&version=NIV

Griffin, R. Morgan. 2015. "10 Natural Depression Treatments." WebMD. WebMD. May 17, 2015. https://www.webmd.com/depression/features/natural-treatments#1. (goals)

Hughes, Locke. 2017. "How to Stop Feeling Anxious Right Now." WebMD. WebMD. March 2, 2017. https://www.webmd.com/mental-health/features/ways-to-reduce-anxiety.

Sleep Foundation. "How Much Sleep Do We Really Need?" https://www.sleepfoundation.org/excessive-sleepiness/support/how-much-sleep-do-we-really-need

CHAPTER 21, TAKE UP YOUR CROSS

Bible Gateway. (2019). *Bible Gateway Passage: John 10:10 – New International Version [Online]* Available at: https://www.biblegateway.com/passage/?search=John+10%3A10+&version=NIV

Bible Gateway. (2019). *Bible Gateway Passage: Joshua 1:9 – New Testament Version [Online]* Available

at: https://www.biblegateway.com/
passage/?search=Joshua+1%3A9&version=NIV

CHAPTER 22, HIGHS AND LOWS

Bible Gateway. (2019). *Bible Gateway Passage: Joshua 1:9 – New Testament Version [Online]* Available at: https://www.biblegateway.com/ passage/?search=Joshua+1%3A9&version=NIV

Bible Gateway. (2019). *Bible Gateway Passage: Romans 8:28 – New Testament Version [Online]* Available at: https://www.biblegateway.com/ passage/?search=romans+8%3A28+&version=NIV

Bible Gateway. (2019). *Bible Gateway Passage: 1 John 4:4 – New Testament Version [Online]* Available at: https://www.biblegateway.com/ passage/?search=1+John+4%3A4&version=NIV

CHAPTER 23, UNCOMFORTABLE

Bible Gateway. (2019). *Bible Gateway Passage: Galatians 5:22-23 – New Testament Version [Online]* Available at: https:// www.biblegateway.com/passage/?search=galatians+5%3A22-23&version=NIV

Bible Gateway. (2019). *Bible Gateway Passage: Luke 5:22 – New Testament Version [Online]* Available at: https://www.biblegateway.com/ passage/?search=Luke+5%3A22&version=NIV

Bible Gateway. (2019). *Bible Gateway Passage: Proverbs 3:5 – New Testament Version [Online]* Available at: https://www.biblegateway.com/ passage/?search=proverbs+3%3A5&version=NIV

Bible Gateway. (2019). *Bible Gateway Passage: Psalm 56:3 – New Testament Version [Online]* Available at: https://www.biblegateway.com/ passage/?search=psalm+56%3A3&version=NIV

CHAPTER 24, PAIN... THEN VICTORY

Bible Gateway. (2019). *Bible Gateway Passage: 1 John 5:4 – New International Version [online]* available at: https://www.biblegateway.com/ passage/?search=1+John+5%3A4&version=NIV

Bible Gateway. (2019) *Bible Gateway Passage: John 11:35 – New International Version [online]* Available at: https://www. biblegateway.com/passage/?search=John+11:35&version=NIV

CHAPTER 25, THE BROKEN ONES

Bible Gateway. (2019). *Bible Gateway Passage: Jeremiah 1:5 – New International Version [online]* Available at: https://www.biblegateway.com/ passage/?search=Jeremiah+1%3A5&version=NIV

Bible Gateway. (2019). *Bible Gateway Passage: 1 Peter 2:16 – New International Version [online]* Available at: https://www.biblegateway.com/ passage/?search=1+Peter+2%3A16&version=NIV

Bible Gateway. (2019). *Bible Gateway Passage: Psalm 34:18 - New International Version* [online] Available at: https://www.biblegateway.com/ passage/?search=psalm+34%3A18+&version=NIV

CHAPTER 26, HEAVEN

Bible Gateway. (2019). *Bible Gateway Passage: Colossians 3:2 - New International Version* [online] Available at: https://www.biblegateway.com/ passage/?search=Colossians+3%3A2+&version=NIV

Bible Gateway. (2019). *Bible Gateway Passage: Revelation 21:3 - New International Version* [online] Available at: https://www.biblegateway.com/ passage/?search=revelation+21%3A3&version=NIV

CHAPTER 27, SNAPCHAT MEMORIES

Bible Gateway. (2019). *Bible Gateway Passage: Proverbs 4:25 - New International Version* [online] Available at: https://www.biblegateway.com/ passage/?search=proverbs+4%3A25&version=NIV

CHAPTER 28, WITH YOU

Bible Gateway. (2019). *Bible Gateway Passage: 2 Chronicles 15:2 - New International Version* [online] Available at: https://www.biblegateway.com/ passage/?search=2+chronicles+15%3A2&version=NIV

Bible Gateway. (2019). *Bible Gateway Passage:*
John 10:27 – New International Version
[online] Available at: https://www.biblegateway.com/
passage/?search=John+10%3A27&version=NIV

CHAPTER 29, OVERWHELMED

Bible Gateway. (2019). *Bible Gateway Passage:*
John 15:11 – New International Version
[online] Available at: https://www.biblegateway.com/
passage/?search=John+15%3A11+&version=NIV

Bible Gateway. (2019). *Bible Gateway Passage:*
Philippians 4:13 – New International Version
[online] Available at: https://www.biblegateway.com/
passage/?search=Philippians+4%3A13&version=NIV

Bible Gateway. (2019). *Bible Gateway Passage:*
Psalm 4:8 – New International Version
[online] Available at https://www.biblegateway.com/
passage/?search=psalm+4%3A8+&version=NIV

CHAPTER 30, IT IS WELL

Bible Gateway. (2019). *Bible Gateway Passage:*
John 11:40 – New International Version
[online] Available at: https://www.biblegateway.com/
passage/?search=John+11%3A40&version=NIV

Bible Gateway. (2019). *Bible Gateway Passage: John 16:33 – New*
International Version [online] Available at:

https://www.biblegateway.com/
passage/?search=John+16%3A33&version=NIV

Bible Gateway. (2019). *Bible Gateway Passage:
Mark 5:34 – New International Version
[online]* Available at: https://www.biblegateway.com/
passage/?search=mark+5%3A34&version=NIV

God bless. Remember, you are so loved, worthy, and amazing. God is going to do amazing things in your life. Never give up.

Made in the USA
Columbia, SC
24 February 2020